Charlotte Mary Yonge

A Short History of France

Charlotte Mary Yonge

A Short History of France

ISBN/EAN: 9783955642433

Auflage: 1

Erscheinungsjahr: 2013

Erscheinungsort: Bremen, Deutschland

@ EHV-History in Access Verlag GmbH, Fahrenheitstr. 1, 28359 Bremen. Alle Rechte beim Verlag und bei den jeweiligen Lizenzgebern.

CONTENTS.

CHAPTER I.	1
THE EARLIER KINGS OF FRANCE.	
CHAPTER II.	19
THE HUNDRED YEARS' WAR.	
CHAPTER III.	33
THE STRUGGLE WITH BURGUNDY.	
CHAPTER IV.	40
THE ITALIAN WARS.	
CHAPTER V.	48
THE WARS OF RELIGION.	
CHAPTER VI.	61
POWER OF THE CROWN.	
CHAPTER VII.	77
THE REVOLUTION.	
CHAPTER VIII.	88
FRANCE SINCE THE REVOLUTION.	

MAP OF FRANCE.

Shewing the Provinces.

MAP OF FRANCE

Shewing the Departments.

CHAPTER I.

THE EARLIER KINGS OF FRANCE.

1. France. — The country we now know as France is the tract of land shut in by the British Channel, the Bay of Biscay, the Pyrenees, the Mediterranean, and the Alps. But this country only gained the name of France by degrees. In the earliest days of which we have any account, it was peopled by the Celts, and it was known to the Romans as part of a larger country which bore the name of Gaul. After all of it, save the north-western moorlands, or what we now call Brittany, had been conquered and settled by the Romans, it was overrun by tribes of the great Teutonic race, the same family to which Englishmen belong. Of these tribes, the Goths settled in the provinces to the south; the Burgundians, in the east, around the Jura; while the Franks, coming over the rivers in its unprotected north-eastern corner, and making themselves masters of a far wider territory, broke up into two kingdoms — that of the Eastern Franks in what is now Germany, and that of the Western Franks reaching from the Rhine to the Atlantic. These Franks subdued all the other Teutonic conquerors of Gaul, while they adopted the religion, the language, and some of the civilization of the Romanized Gauls who became their subjects. Under the second Frankish dynasty, the Empire was renewed in the West, where it had been for a time put an end to by these Teutonic invasions, and the then Frankish king, Charles the Great, took his place as Emperor at its head. But in the time of his grandsons the various kingdoms and nations of which the Empire was composed, fell apart again under different descendants of his. One of these, *Charles the Bald*, was made King of

the Western Franks in what was termed the Neustrian, or "not eastern," kingdom, from which the present France has sprung. This kingdom in name covered all the country west of the Upper Meuse, but practically the Neustrian king had little power south of the Loire; and the Celts of Brittany were never included in it.

2. The House of Paris. — The great danger which this Neustrian kingdom had to meet came from the Northmen, or as they were called in England the Danes. These ravaged in Neustria as they ravaged in England; and a large part of the northern coast, including the mouth of the Seine, was given by Charles the Bald to Rolf or Rollo, one of their leaders, whose land became known as the Northman's land, or Normandy. What most checked the ravages of these pirates was the resistance of Paris, a town which commanded the road along the river Seine; and it was in defending the city of Paris from the Northmen, that a warrior named Robert the Strong gained the trust and affection of the inhabitants of the Neustrian kingdom. He and his family became Counts (*i.e.*, judges and protectors) of Paris, and Dukes (or leaders) of the Franks. Three generations of them were really great men — Robert the Strong, Odo, and Hugh the White; and when the descendants of Charles the Great had died out, a Duke of the Franks, *Hugh Capet*, was in 987 crowned King of the Franks. All the after kings of France down to Louis Philippe were descendants of Hugh Capet. By this change, however, he gained little in real power; for, though he claimed to rule over the whole country of the Neustrian Franks, his authority was little heeded, save in the domain which he had possessed as Count of Paris, including the cities of Paris, Orleans, Amiens, and Rheims (the coronation place). He was guardian, too, of the great Abbeys of

St. Denys and St. Martin of Tours. The Duke of Normandy and the Count of Anjou to the west, the Count of Flanders to the north, the Count of Champagne to the east, and the Duke of Aquitaine to the south, paid him homage, but were the only actual rulers in their own domains.

3. The Kingdom of Hugh Capet. — The language of Hugh's kingdom was clipped Latin; the peasantry and townsmen were mostly Gaulish; the nobles were almost entirely Frank. There was an understanding that the king could only act by their consent, and must be chosen by them; but matters went more by old custom and the right of the strongest than by any law. A Salic law, so called from the place whence the Franks had come, was supposed to exist; but this had never been used by their subjects, whose law remained that of the old Roman Empire. Both of these systems of law, however, fell into disuse, and were replaced by rude bodies of "customs," which gradually grew up. The habits of the time were exceedingly rude and ferocious. The Franks had been the fiercest and most untamable of all the Teutonic nations, and only submitted themselves to the influence of Christianity and civilization from the respect which the Roman Empire inspired. Charles the Great had tried to bring in Roman cultivation, but we find him reproaching the young Franks in his schools with letting themselves be surpassed by the Gauls, whom they despised; and in the disorders that followed his death, barbarism increased again. The convents alone kept up any remnants of culture; but as the fury of the Northmen was chiefly directed to them, numbers had been destroyed, and there was more ignorance and wretchedness than at any other time. In the duchy of Aquitaine, much more of the old Roman civilization survived, both among the cities and the nobility; and

the Normans, newly settled in the north, had brought with them the vigour of their race. They had taken up such dead or dying culture as they found in France, and were carrying it further, so as in some degree to awaken their neighbours. Kings and their great vassals could generally read and write, and understand the Latin in which all records were made, but few except the clergy studied at all. There were schools in convents, and already at Paris a university was growing up for the study of theology, grammar, law, philosophy, and music, the sciences which were held to form a course of education. The doctors of these sciences lectured; the scholars of low degree lived, begged, and struggled as best they could; and gentlemen were lodged with clergy, who served as a sort of private tutors.

4. Earlier Kings of the House of Paris. — Neither Hugh nor the next three kings (*Robert*, 996-1031; *Henry*, 1031-1060; *Philip*, 1060-1108) were able men, and they were almost helpless among the fierce nobles of their own domain, and the great counts and dukes around them. Castles were built of huge strength, and served as nests of plunderers, who preyed on travellers and made war on each other, grievously tormenting one another's "villeins" — as the peasants were termed. Men could travel nowhere in safety, and horrid ferocity and misery prevailed. The first three kings were good and pious men, but too weak to deal with their ruffian nobles. *Robert, called the Pious*, was extremely devout, but weak. He became embroiled with the Pope on account of having married Bertha — a lady pronounced to be within the degrees of affinity prohibited by the Church. He was excommunicated, but held out till there was a great religious reaction, produced by the belief that the world would end in 1000. In this expectation many

persons left their land untilled, and the consequence was a terrible famine, followed by a pestilence; and the misery of France was probably unequalled in this reign, when it was hardly possible to pass safely from one to another of the three royal cities, Paris, Orleans, and Tours. Beggars swarmed, and the king gave to them everything he could lay his hands on, and even winked at their stealing gold off his dress, to the great wrath of a second wife, the imperious Constance of Provence, who, coming from the more luxurious and corrupt south, hated and despised the roughness and asceticism of her husband. She was a fierce and passionate woman, and brought an element of cruelty into the court. In this reign the first instance of persecution to the death for heresy took place. The victim had been the queen's confessor; but so far was she from pitying him that she struck out one of his eyes with her staff, as he was led past her to the hut where he was shut in and burnt. On Robert's death Constance took part against her son, *Henry I.*, on behalf of his younger brother, but Henry prevailed. During his reign the clergy succeeded in proclaiming what was called the Truce of God, which forbade war and bloodshed at certain seasons of the year and on certain days of the week, and made churches and clerical lands places of refuge and sanctuary, which often indeed protected the lawless, but which also saved the weak and oppressed. It was during these reigns that the Papacy was beginning the great struggle for temporal power, and freedom from the influence of the Empire, which resulted in the increased independence and power of the clergy. The religious fervour which had begun with the century led to the foundation of many monasteries, and to much grand church architecture. In the reign of *Philip I.*, William, Duke of Normandy, obtained the kingdom of England, and thus became far more powerful than his suzerain, the King of France, a weak man of vicious habits, who lay for many years of his life under sentence of excommunication for an adulterous marriage with Bertrade de Montfort, Countess of Anjou. The power of the king and of the law was probably at the very lowest ebb during the time of Philip I., though minds and manners were less debased than in the former century.

5. The First Crusade (1095 — 1100). — Pilgrimage to the Holy Land had now become one great means by which the men of the West sought pardon for their sins. Jerusalem had long been held by the Arabs, who had treated the pilgrims well; but these had been conquered by a fierce Turcoman tribe, who robbed and oppressed the pilgrims. Peter the Hermit, returning from a pilgrimage, persuaded Pope Urban II. that it would be well to stir up Christendom to drive back the Moslem power, and deliver Jerusalem and the holy places. Urban II. accordingly, when holding a council at Clermont, in Auvergne, permitted Peter to describe in glowing words the miseries of pilgrims and the profanation of the holy places. Cries broke out, "God wills it!" and multitudes thronged to receive crosses cut out in cloth, which were fastened to the shoulder, and pledged the wearer to the holy war or crusade, as it was called. Philip I. took no interest in the cause, but his brother Hugh, Count of Vermandois, Stephen, Count of Blois, Robert, Duke of Normandy, and Raymond, Count of Toulouse, joined the expedition, which was made under Godfrey of Bouillon, Duke of Lower Lorraine, or what we now call the Netherlands. The crusade proved successful; Jerusalem was gained, and a kingdom of detached cities and forts was founded in Palestine, of which Godfrey became the first king. The whole of the West was sup-

posed to keep up the defence of the Holy Land, but, in fact, most of those who went as armed pilgrims were either French, Normans, or Aquitanians; and the men of the East called all alike Franks. Two orders of monks, who were also knights, became the permanent defenders of the kingdom — the Knights of St. John, also called Hospitallers, because they also lodged pilgrims and tended the sick; and the Knights Templars. Both had establishments in different countries in Europe, where youths were trained to the rules of their order. The old custom of solemnly girding a young warrior with his sword was developing into a system by which the nobly born man was trained through the ranks of page and squire to full knighthood, and made to take vows which bound him to honourable customs to equals, though, unhappily, no account was taken of his inferiors.

6. Louis VI. and VII. — Philip's son, *Louis VI., or the Fat*, was the first able man whom the line of Hugh Capet had produced since it mounted the throne. He made the first attempt at curbing the nobles, assisted by Suger, the Abbot of St. Denys. The only possibility of doing this was to obtain the aid of one party of nobles against another; and when any unusually flagrant offence had been committed, Louis called together the nobles, bishops, and abbots of his domain, and obtained their consent and assistance in making war on the guilty man, and overthrowing his castle, thus, in some degree, lessening the sense of utter impunity which had caused so many violences and such savage recklessness. He also permitted a few of the cities to purchase the right of self-government, and freedom from the ill usage of the counts, who, from their guardians, had become their tyrants; but in this he seems not to have been so much guided by any fixed principle, as by his private interests and feelings

towards the individual city or lord in question. However, the royal authority had begun to be respected by 1137, when Louis VI. died, having just effected the marriage of his son, *Louis VII.*, with Eleanor, the heiress of the Dukes of Aquitaine — thus hoping to make the crown really more powerful than the great princes who owed it homage. At this time lived the great St. Bernard, Abbot of Clairvaux, who had a wonderful influence over men's minds. It was a time of much thought and speculation, and Peter Abailard, an able student of the Paris University, held a controversy with Bernard, in which we see the first struggle between intellect and authority. Bernard roused the young king, Louis VII., to go on the second crusade, which was undertaken by the Emperor and the other princes of Europe to relieve the distress of the kingdom of Palestine. France had no navy, so the war was by land, through the rugged hills of Asia Minor, where the army was almost destroyed by the Saracens. Though Louis did reach Palestine, it was with weakened forces; he could effect nothing by his campaign, and Eleanor, who had accompanied him, seems to have been entirely corrupted by the evil habits of the Franks settled in the East. Soon after his return, Louis dissolved his marriage; and Eleanor became the wife of Henry, Count of Anjou, who soon after inherited the kingdom of England as our Henry II., as well as the duchy of Normandy, and betrothed his third son to the heiress of Brittany. Eleanor's marriage seemed to undo all that Louis VI. had done in raising the royal power; for Henry completely overshadowed Louis, whose only resource was in feeble endeavours to take part against him in his many family quarrels. The whole reign of Louis the Young, the title that adhered to him on account of his simple, childish nature, is only a record of weakness and disaster, till he died in 1180. What life went on in France, went on principally in the south. The lands of Aquitaine and Provence had never dropped the old classical love of poetry and art. A softer form of broken Latin was then spoken, and the art of minstrelsy was frequent among all ranks. Poets were called troubadours and *trouvères* (finders). Courts of love were held, where there were competitions in poetry, the prize being a golden violet; and many of the bravest warriors were also distinguished troubadours — among them the elder sons of Queen Eleanor. There was much license of manners, much turbulence; and as the Aquitanians hated Angevin rule, the troubadours never ceased to stir up the sons of Henry II. against him.

7. Philip II. (1180 — 1223). — Powerful in fact as Henry II. was, it was his gathering so large a part of France under his rule which was, in the end, to build up the greatness of the French kings. What had held them in check was the existence of the great fiefs or provinces, each with its own line of dukes or counts, and all practically independent of the king. But now nearly all the provinces of southern and western France were gathered into the hand of a single ruler; and though he was a Frenchman in blood, yet, as he was King of England, this ruler seemed to his French subjects no Frenchman, but a foreigner. They began therefore to look to the French king to free them from a foreign ruler; and the son of Louis VII., called *Philip Augustus*, was ready to take advantage of their disposition. Philip was a really able man, making up by address for want of personal courage. He set himself to lower the power of the house of Anjou and increase that of the house of Paris. As a boy he had watched conferences between his father and Henry under the great elm of Gisors, on the borders of Normandy, and

seeing his father overreached, he laid up a store of hatred to the rival king. As soon as he had the power, he cut down the elm, which was so large that 300 horsemen could be sheltered under its branches. He supported the sons of Henry II. in their rebellions, and was always the bitter foe of the head of the family. Philip assumed the cross in 1187, on the tidings of the loss of Jerusalem, and in 1190 joined Richard I. of England at Messina, where they wintered, and then sailed for St. Jean d'Acre. After this city was taken, Philip returned to France, where he continued to profit by the crimes and dissensions of the Angevins, and gained, both as their enemy and as King of France. When Richard's successor, John, murdered Arthur, the heir of the dukedom of Brittany and claimant of both Anjou and Normandy, Philip took advantage of the general indignation to hold a court of peers, in which John, on his non-appearance, was adjudged to have forfeited his fiefs. In the war which followed and ended in 1204, Philip not only gained the great Norman dukedom, which gave him the command of Rouen and of the mouth of the Seine, as well as Anjou, Maine, and Poitou, the countries which held the Loire in their power, but established the precedent that a crown vassal was amenable to justice, and might be made to forfeit his lands. What he had won by the sword he held by wisdom and good government. Seeing that the cities were capable of being made to balance the power of the nobles, he granted them privileges which caused him to be esteemed their best friend, and he promoted all improvements. Though once laid under an interdict by Pope Innocent III. for an unlawful marriage, Philip usually followed the policy which gained for the Kings of France the title of "Most Christian King." The real meaning of this was that he should always support the Pope against the Emperor, and in return be allowed more than ordinary power over his clergy. The great feudal vassals of eastern France, with a strong instinct that he was their enemy, made a league with the Emperor Otto IV. and his uncle King John, against Philip Augustus. John attacked him in the south, and was repulsed by Philip's son, Louis, called the "Lion;" while the king himself, backed by the burghers of his chief cities, gained at Bouvines, over Otto, the first real French victory, in 1214, thus establishing the power of the crown. Two years later, Louis the Lion, who had married John's niece, Blanche of Castile, was invited by the English barons to become their king on John's refusing to be bound by the Great Charter; and Philip saw his son actually in possession of London at the time of the death of the last of the sons of his enemy, Henry II. On John's death, however, the barons preferred his child to the French prince, and fell away from Louis, who was forced to return to France.

8. The Albigenses (1203 — 1240). — The next great step in the building up of the French kingdom was made by taking advantage of a religious strife in the south. The lands near the Mediterranean still had much of the old Roman cultivation, and also of the old corruption, and here arose a sect called the Albigenses, who held opinions other than those of the Church on the origin of evil. Pope Innocent III., after sending some of the order of friars freshly established by the Spaniard, Dominic, to preach to them in vain, declared them as great enemies of the faith as Mahometans, and proclaimed a crusade against them and their chief supporter, Raymond, Count of Toulouse. Shrewd old King Philip merely permitted this crusade; but the dislike of the north of France to the south made hosts of adventurers flock to the banner of its leader, Simon de Montfort, a Norman baron,

devout and honourable, but harsh and pitiless. Dreadful execution was done; the whole country was laid waste, and Raymond reduced to such distress that Peter I., King of Aragon, who was regarded as the natural head of the southern races, came to his aid, but was defeated and slain at the battle of Muret. After this Raymond was forced to submit, but such hard terms were forced on him that his people revolted. His country was granted to De Montfort, who laid siege to Toulouse, and was killed before he could take the city. The war was then carried on by *Louis the Lion*, who had succeeded his father as Louis VIII. in 1223, though only to reign three years, as he died of a fever caught in a southern campaign in 1226. His widow, Blanche, made peace in the name of her son, *Louis IX.*, and Raymond was forced to give his only daughter in marriage to one of her younger sons. On their death, the county of Toulouse lapsed to the crown, which thus became possessor of all southern France, save Guienne, which still remained to the English kings. But the whole of the district once peopled by the Albigenses had been so much wasted as never to recover its prosperity, and any cropping up of their opinions was guarded against by the establishment of the Inquisition, which appointed Dominican friars to *inquire* into and exterminate all that differed from the Church. At the same time the order of St. Francis did much to instruct and quicken the consciences of the people; and at the universities — especially that of Paris — a great advance both in thought and learning was made. Louis IX.'s confessor, Henry de Sorbonne, founded, for the study of divinity, the college which was known by his name, and whose decisions were afterwards received as of paramount authority.

9. The Parliament of Paris. — France had a wise ruler in Blanche, and a still better one in her son, *Louis*

IX., who is better known as *St. Louis*, and who was a really good and great man. He was the first to establish the Parliament of Paris — a court consisting of the great feudal vassals, lay and ecclesiastical, who held of the king direct, and who had to try all causes. They much disliked giving such attendance, and a certain number of men trained to the law were added to them to guide the decisions. The Parliament was thus only a court of justice and an office for registering wills and edicts. The representative assembly of France was called the States-General, and consisted of all estates of the realm, but was only summoned in time of emergency. Louis IX. was the first king to bring nobles of the highest rank to submit to the judgment of Parliament when guilty of a crime. Enguerrand de Coucy, one of the proudest nobles of France, who had hung two Flemish youths for killing a rabbit, was sentenced to death. The penalty was commuted, but the principle was established. Louis's uprightness and wisdom gained him honour and love everywhere, and he was always remembered as sitting under the great oak at Vincennes, doing equal justice to rich and poor. Louis was equally upright in his dealings with foreign powers. He would not take advantage of the weakness of Henry III. of England to attack his lands in Guienne, though he maintained the right of France to Normandy as having been forfeited by King John. So much was he respected that he was called in to judge between Henry and his barons, respecting the oaths exacted from the king by the Mad Parliament. His decision in favour of Henry was probably an honest one; but he was misled by the very different relations of the French and English kings to their nobles, who in France maintained lawlessness and violence, while in England they were struggling for law and order. Throughout the struggles between the Popes and the Emperor Frederick II., Louis would not be induced to assist in a persecution of the Emperor which he considered unjust, nor permit one of his sons to accept the kingdom of Apulia and Sicily, when the Pope declared that Frederick had forfeited it. He could not, however, prevent his brother Charles, Count of Anjou, from accepting it; for Charles had married Beatrice, heiress of the imperial fief of Provence, and being thus independent of his brother Louis, was able to establish a branch of the French royal family on the throne at Naples. The reign of St. Louis was a time of much progress and improvement. There were great scholars and thinkers at all the universities. Romance and poetry were flourishing, and influencing people's habits, so that courtesy, *i.e.* the manners taught in castle courts, was softening the demeanour of knights and nobles. Architecture was at its most beautiful period, as is seen, above all, in the Sainte Chapelle at Paris. This was built by Louis IX. to receive a gift of the Greek Emperor, namely, a thorn, which was believed to be from the crown of thorns. It is one of the most perfect buildings in existence.

10. Crusade of Louis IX. — Unfortunately, Louis, during a severe illness, made a vow to go on a crusade. His first fulfilment of this vow was made early in his reign, in 1250, when his mother was still alive to undertake the regency. His attempt was to attack the heart of the Saracen power in Egypt, and he effected a landing and took the city of Damietta. There he left his queen, and advanced on Cairo; but near Mansourah he found himself entangled in the canals of the Nile, and with a great army of Mamelukes in front. A ford was found, and the English Earl of Salisbury, who had brought a troop to join the crusade, advised that the first to cross should wait and guard the passage of the next. But the king's brother, Robert, Count

of Artois, called this cowardice. The earl was stung, and declared he would be as forward among the foe as any Frenchman. They both charged headlong, were enclosed by the enemy, and slain; and though the king at last put the Mamelukes to flight, his loss was dreadful. The Nile rose and cut off his return. He lost great part of his troops from sickness, and was horribly harassed by the Mamelukes, who threw among his host a strange burning missile, called Greek fire; and he was finally forced to surrender himself as a prisoner at Mansourah, with all his army. He obtained his release by giving up Damietta, and paying a heavy ransom. After twenty years, in 1270, he attempted another crusade, which was still more unfortunate, for he landed at Tunis to wait for his brother to arrive from Sicily, apparently on some delusion of favourable dispositions on the part of the Bey. Sickness broke out in the camp, and the king, his daughter, and his third son all died of fever; and so fatal was the expedition, that his son Philip III. returned to France escorting five coffins, those of his father, his brother, his sister and her husband, and his own wife and child.

11. Philip the Fair. — The reign of *Philip III.* was very short. The insolence and cruelty of the Provençals in Sicily had provoked the natives to a massacre known as the Sicilian Vespers, and they then called in the King of Aragon, who finally obtained the island, as a separate kingdom from that on the Italian mainland where Charles of Anjou and his descendants still reigned. While fighting his uncle's battles on the Pyrenees, and besieging Gerona, Philip III. caught a fever, and died on his way home in 1285. His successor, *Philip IV., called the Fair*, was crafty, cruel, and greedy, and made the Parliament of Paris the instrument of his violence and exactions, which he

carried out in the name of the law. To prevent Guy de Dampierre, Count of Flanders, from marrying his daughter to the son of Edward I. of England, he invited her and her father to his court, and threw them both into prison, while he offered his own daughter Isabel to Edward of Carnarvon in her stead. The Scottish wars prevented Edward I. from taking up the cause of Guy; but the Pope, Boniface VIII., a man of a fierce temper, though of a great age, loudly called on Philip to do justice to Flanders, and likewise blamed in unmeasured terms his exactions from the clergy, his debasement of the coinage, and his foul and vicious life. Furious abuse passed on both sides. Philip availed himself of a flaw in the Pope's election to threaten him with deposition, and in return was excommunicated. He then sent a French knight named William de Nogaret, with Sciarra Colonna, a turbulent Roman, the hereditary enemy of Boniface, and a band of savage mercenary soldiers to Anagni, where the Pope then was, to force him to recall the sentence, apparently intending them to act like the murderers of Becket. The old man's dignity, however, overawed them at the moment, and they retired without laying hands on him, but the shock he had undergone caused his death a few days later. His successor was poisoned almost immediately on his election, being known to be adverse to Philip. Parties were equally balanced in the conclave; but Philip's friends advised him to buy over to his interest one of his supposed foes, whom they would then unite in choosing. Bertrand de Goth, Archbishop of Bordeaux, was the man, and in a secret interview promised Philip to fulfil six conditions if he were made Pope by his interest. These were: 1st, the reconciliation of Philip with the Church; 2nd, that of his agents; 3rd, a grant to the king of a tenth of all clerical property for five years; 4th, the restoration of the Colonna family to Rome; 5th, the censure of Boniface's memory. These five were carried out by Clement V., as he called himself, as soon as he was on the Papal throne; the sixth remained a secret, but was probably the destruction of the Knights Templars. This order of military monks had been created for the defence of the crusading kingdom of Jerusalem, and had acquired large possessions in Europe. Now that their occupation in the East was gone, they were hated and dreaded by the kings, and Philip was resolved on their wholesale destruction.

12. The Papacy at Avignon. — Clement had never quitted France, but had gone through the ceremonies of his installation at Lyons; and Philip, fearing that in Italy he would avoid carrying out the scheme for the ruin of the Templars, had him conducted to Avignon, a city of the Empire which belonged to the Angevin King of Naples, as Count of Provence, and there for eighty years the Papal court remained. As they were thus settled close to the French frontier, the Popes became almost vassals of France; and this added greatly to the power and renown of the French kings. How real their hold on the Papacy was, was shown in the ruin of the Templars. The order was now abandoned by the Pope, and its knights were invited in large numbers to Paris, under pretence of arranging a crusade. Having been thus entrapped, they were accused of horrible and monstrous crimes, and torture elicited a few supposed confessions. They were then tried by the Inquisition, and the greater number were put to death by fire, the Grand Master last of all, while their lands were seized by the king. They seem to have been really a fierce, arrogant, and oppressive set of men, or else there must have been some endeavour to save them, belonging, as most of them did, to noble French families. The "Pest of

France," as Dante calls Philip the Fair, was now the most formidable prince in Europe. He contrived to annex to his dominions the city of Lyons, hitherto an imperial city under its archbishop. Philip died in 1314; and his three sons — *Louis X.*, *Philip V.*, and *Charles IV.*, — were as cruel and harsh as himself, but without his talent, and brought the crown and people to disgrace and misery. Each reigned a few years and then died, leaving only daughters, and the question arose whether the inheritance should go to females. When Louis X. died, in 1316, his brother Philip, after waiting for the birth of a posthumous child who only lived a few days, took the crown, and the Parliament then declared that the law of the old Salian Franks had been against the inheritance of women. By this newly discovered Salic law, Charles IV., the third brother, reigned on Philip's death; but the kingdom of Navarre having accrued to the family through their grandmother, and not being subject to the Salic law, went to the eldest daughter of Louis X., Jane, wife of the Count of Evreux.

CHAPTER II.

THE HUNDRED YEARS' WAR.

1. Wars of Edward III. — By the Salic law, as the lawyers called it, the crown was given, on the death of Charles IV., to *Philip, Count of Valois*, son to a brother of Philip IV., but it was claimed by Edward III. of England as son of the daughter of Philip IV. Edward contented himself, however, with the mere assertion of his pretensions, until Philip exasperated him by attacks on the borders of Guienne, which the French kings had long been coveting to complete their possession of the south, and by demanding the surrender of Robert of Artois, who, being disappointed in his claim to the county of Artois by the judgment of the Parliament of Paris, was practising by sorcery on the life of the King of France. Edward then declared war, and his supposed right caused a century of warfare between France and England, in which the broken, down-trodden state of the French peasantry gave England an immense advantage. The knights and squires were fairly matched; but while the English yeomen were strong, staunch, and trustworthy, the French were useless, and only made a defeat worse by plundering the fallen on each side alike. The war began in Flanders, where Philip took the part of the count, whose tyrannies had caused his expulsion. Edward was called in to the aid of the citizens of Ghent by their leader Jacob van Arteveldt; and gained a great victory over the French fleet at Sluys, but with no important result. At the same time the two kings took opposite sides in the war of the succession in Brittany, each defending the claim most inconsistent with his own pretensions to the French crown — Edward upholding the male heir, John de Montfort, and

Philip the direct female representative, the wife of Charles de Blois.

2. Creçy and Poitiers. — Further difficulties arose through Charles the Bad, King of Navarre and Count of Evreux, who was always on the watch to assert his claim to the French throne through his mother, the daughter of Louis X., and was much hated and distrusted by Philip VI. and his son John, Duke of Normandy. Fearing the disaffection of the Norman and Breton nobles, Philip invited a number of them to a tournament at Paris, and there had them put to death after a hasty form of trial, thus driving their kindred to join his enemies. One of these offended Normans, Godfrey of Harcourt, invited Edward to Normandy, where he landed, and having consumed his supplies was on his march to Flanders, when Philip, with the whole strength of the kingdom, endeavoured to intercept him at *Creçy* in Picardy, in 1348. Philip was utterly incapable as a general; his knights were wrongheaded and turbulent, and absolutely cut down their own Genoese hired archers for being in their way. The defeat was total. Philip rode away to Amiens, and Edward laid siege to Calais. The place was so strong that he was forced to blockade it, and Philip had time to gather another army to attempt its relief; but the English army were so posted that he could not attack them without great loss. He retreated, and the men of Calais surrendered, Edward insisting that six burghers should bring him the keys with ropes round their necks, to submit themselves to him. Six offered themselves, but their lives were spared, and they were honourably treated. Edward expelled all the French, and made Calais an English settlement. A truce followed, chiefly in consequence of the ravages of the Black Death, which swept off multitudes throughout Europe, a pestilence apparently bred by filth, famine,

and all the miseries of war and lawlessness, but which spared no ranks. It had scarcely ceased before Philip died, in 1350. His son, *John*, was soon involved in a fresh war with England by the intrigues of Charles the Bad, and in 1356 advanced southwards to check the Prince of Wales, who had come out of Guienne on a plundering expedition. The French were again totally routed at Poitiers, and the king himself, with his third son, Philip, were made prisoners and carried to London with most of the chief nobles.

3. The Jacquerie. — The calls made on their vassals by these captive nobles to supply their ransoms brought the misery to a height. The salt tax, or *gabelle*, which was first imposed to meet the expenses of the war, was only paid by those who were neither clergy nor nobles, and the general saying was — "Jacques Bonhomme (the nickname for the peasant) has a broad back, let him bear all the burthens." Either by the king, the feudal lords, the clergy, or the bands of men-at-arms who roved through the country, selling themselves to any prince who would employ them, the wretched people were stripped of everything, and used to hide in holes and caves from ill-usage or insult, till they broke out in a rebellion called the Jacquerie, and whenever they could seize a castle revenged themselves, like the brutes they had been made, on those within it. Taxation was so levied by the king's officers as to be frightfully oppressive, and corruption reigned everywhere. As the king was in prison, and his heir, Charles, had fled ignominiously from Poitiers, the citizens of Paris hoped to effect a reform, and rose with their provost-marshal, Stephen Marcel, at their head, threatened Charles, and slew two of his officers before his eyes. On their demand the States-General were convoked, and made wholesome regulations as to the manner of collecting the

taxes, but no one, except perhaps Marcel, had any real zeal or public spirit. Charles the Bad, of Navarre, who had pretended to espouse their cause, betrayed it; the king declared the decisions of the States-General null and void; and the crafty management of his son prevented any union between the malcontents. The gentry rallied, and put down the Jacquerie with horrible cruelty and revenge. The burghers of Paris found that Charles the Bad only wanted to gain the throne, and Marcel would have proclaimed him; but those who thought him even worse than his cousins of Valois admitted the other Charles, by whom Marcel and his partisans were put to death. The attempt at reform thus ended in talk and murder, and all fell back into the same state of misery and oppression.

4. The Peace of Bretigny. — This Charles, eldest son of John, obtained by purchase the imperial fief of Vienne, of which the counts had always been called Dauphins, a title thenceforth borne by the heir apparent of the kingdom. His father's captivity and the submission of Paris left him master of the realm; but he did little to defend it when Edward III. again attacked it, and in 1360 he was forced to bow to the terms which the English king demanded as the price of peace. The Peace of Bretigny permitted King John to ransom himself, but resigned to England the sovereignty over the duchy of Aquitaine, and left Calais and Ponthieu in the hands of Edward III. John died in 1364, before his ransom was paid, and his son mounted the throne as *Charles V.* Charles showed himself from this time a wary, able man, and did much to regain what had been lost by craftily watching his opportunity. The war went on between the allies of each party, though the French and English kings professed to be at peace; and at the battle of Cocherel, in 1364, Charles the Bad was defeated, and

forced to make peace with France. On the other hand, the French party in Brittany, led by Charles de Blois and the gallant Breton knight, Bertrand du Guesclin, were routed, the same year, by the English party under Sir John Chandos; Charles de Blois was killed, and the house of Montfort established in the duchy. These years of war had created a dreadful class of men, namely, hired soldiers of all nations, who, under some noted leader, sold their services to whatever prince might need them, under the name of Free Companies, and when unemployed lived by plunder. The peace had only let these wretches loose on the peasants. Some had seized castles, whence they could plunder travellers; others roamed the country, preying on the miserable peasants, who, fleeced as they were by king, barons, and clergy, were tortured and murdered by these ruffians, so that many lived in holes in the ground that their dwellings might not attract attention. Bertrand du Guesclin offered the king to relieve the country from these Free Companies by leading them to assist the Castilians against their tyrannical king, Peter the Cruel. Edward, the Black Prince, who was then acting as Governor of Aquitaine, took, however, the part of Peter, and defeated Du Guesclin at the battle of Navarete, on the Ebro, in 1367.

5. Renewal of the War. — This expedition ruined the prince's health, and exhausted his treasury. A hearth-tax was laid on the inhabitants of Aquitaine, and they appealed against it to the King of France, although, by the Peace of Bretigny, he had given up all right to hear appeals as suzerain. The treaty, however, was still not formally settled, and on this ground Charles received their complaint. The war thus began again, and the sword of the Constable of France — the highest military dignity of the realm — was given to Du Guesclin, but only on condition that he would

avoid pitched battles, and merely harass the English and take their castles. This policy was so strictly followed, that the Duke of Lancaster was allowed to march from Brittany to Gascony without meeting an enemy in the field; and when King Edward III. made his sixth and last invasion, nearly to the walls of Paris, he was only turned back by famine, and by a tremendous thunderstorm, which made him believe that Heaven was against him. Du Guesclin died while besieging a castle, and such was his fame that the English captain would place the keys in no hand but that of his corpse. The Constable's sword was given to Oliver de Clisson, also a Breton, and called the "Butcher," because he gave no quarter to the English in revenge for the death of his brother. The Bretons were, almost to a man, of the French party, having been offended by the insolence and oppression of the English; and John de Montfort, after clinging to the King of England as long as possible, was forced to make his peace at length with Charles. Charles V. had nearly regained all that had been lost, when, in 1380 his death left the kingdom to his son.

6. House of Burgundy. — *Charles VI.* was a boy of nine years old, motherless, and beset with ambitious uncles. These uncles were Louis, Duke of Anjou, to whom Queen Joanna, the last of the earlier Angevin line in Naples, bequeathed her rights; John, Duke of Berry, a weak time-server; and Philip, the ablest and most honest of the three. His grandmother Joan, the wife of Philip VI., had been heiress of the duchy and county of Burgundy, and these now became his inheritance, giving him the richest part of France. By still better fortune he had married Margaret, the only child of Louis, Count of Flanders. Flanders contained the great cloth-manufacturing towns of Europe — Ghent, Bruges, Ypres, etc., all wealthy and independ-

ent, and much inclined to close alliance with England, whence they obtained their wool, while their counts were equally devoted to France. Just as Count Louis II. had, for his lawless rapacity, been driven out of Ghent by Jacob van Arteveldt, so his son, Louis III., was expelled by Philip van Arteveldt, son to Jacob. Charles had been disgusted by Louis's coarse violence, and would not help him; but after the old king's death, Philip of Burgundy used his influence in the council to conduct the whole power of France to Flanders, where Arteveldt was defeated and trodden to death in the battle of Rosbecque, in 1382. On the count's death, Philip succeeded him as Count of Flanders in right of his wife; and thus was laid the foundation of the powerful and wealthy house of Burgundy, which for four generations almost overshadowed the crown of France.

7. Insanity of Charles VI. — The Constable, Clisson, was much hated by the Duke of Brittany, and an attack which was made on him in the streets of Paris was clearly traced to Montfort. The young king, who was much attached to Clisson, set forth to exact punishment. On his way, a madman rushed out of a forest and called out, "King, you are betrayed!" Charles was much frightened, and further seems to have had a sunstroke, for he at once became insane. He recovered for a time; but at Christmas, while he and five others were dancing, disguised as wild men, their garments of pitched flax caught fire. Four were burnt, and the shock brought back the king's madness. He became subject to fits of insanity of longer or shorter duration, and in their intervals he seems to have been almost imbecile. No provision had then been made for the contingency of a mad king. The condition of the country became worse than ever, and power was grasped at by whoever could obtain it. Of the king's three un-

cles, the Duke of Anjou and his sons were generally engrossed by a vain struggle to obtain Naples; the Duke of Berry was dull and weak; and the chief struggle for influence was between Philip of Burgundy and his son, John the Fearless, on the one hand, and on the other the king's wife, Isabel of Bavaria, and his brother Louis, Duke of Orleans, who was suspected of being her lover; while the unhappy king and his little children were left in a wretched state, often scarcely provided with clothes or food.

8. Burgundians and Armagnacs. — Matters grew worse after the death of Duke Philip in 1404; and in 1407, just after a seeming reconciliation, the Duke of Orleans was murdered in the streets of Paris by servants of John the Fearless. Louis of Orleans had been a vain, foolish man, heedless of all save his own pleasure, but his death increased the misery of France through the long and deadly struggle for vengeance that followed. The king was helpless, and the children of the Duke of Orleans were young; but their cause was taken up by a Gascon noble, Bernard, Count of Armagnac, whose name the party took. The Duke of Burgundy was always popular in Paris, where the people, led by the Guild of Butchers, were so devoted to him that he ventured to have a sermon preached at the university, justifying the murder. There was again a feeble attempt at reform made by the burghers; but, as before, the more violent and lawless were guilty of such excesses that the opposite party were called in to put them down. The Armagnacs were admitted into Paris, and took a terrible vengeance on the Butchers and on all adherents of Burgundy, in the name of the Dauphin Louis, the king's eldest son, a weak, dissipated youth, who was entirely led by the Count of Armagnac.

9. Invasion of Henry V. — All this time the war with England had smouldered on, only broken by brief truces; and when France was in this wretched state Henry V. renewed the claim of Edward III., and in 1415 landed before Harfleur. After delaying till he had taken the city, the dauphin called together the whole nobility of the kingdom, and advanced against Henry, who, like Edward III., had been obliged to leave Normandy and march towards Calais in search of supplies. The armies met at Agincourt, where, though the French greatly outnumbered the English, the skill of Henry and the folly and confusion of the dauphin's army led to a total defeat, and the captivity of half the chief men in France of the Armagnac party — among them the young Duke of Orleans. It was Henry V.'s policy to treat France, not as a conquest, but as an inheritance; and he therefore refused to let these captives be ransomed till he should have reduced the country to obedience, while he treated all the places that submitted to him with great kindness. The Duke of Burgundy held aloof from the contest, and the Armagnacs, who ruled in Paris, were too weak or too careless to send aid to Rouen, which was taken by Henry after a long siege. The Dauphin Louis died in 1417; his next brother, John, who was more inclined to Burgundy, did not survive him a year; and the third brother, Charles, a mere boy, was in the hands of the Armagnacs. In 1418 their reckless misuse of power provoked the citizens of Paris into letting in the Burgundians, when an unspeakably horrible massacre took place. Bernard of Armagnac himself was killed; his naked corpse, scored with his red cross, was dragged about the streets; and men, women, and even infants of his party were slaughtered pitilessly. Tanneguy Duchatel, one of his partisans, carried off the dauphin; but the queen, weary of Armagnac inso-

lence, had joined the Burgundian party.

10. Treaty of Troyes. — Meanwhile Henry V. continued to advance, and John of Burgundy felt the need of joining the whole strength of France against him, and made overtures to the dauphin. Duchatel, either fearing to be overshadowed by his power, or else in revenge for Orleans and Armagnac, no sooner saw that a reconciliation was likely to take place, than he murdered John the Fearless before the dauphin's eyes, at a conference on the bridge of Montereau-sur-Yonne (1419). John's wound was said to be the hole which let the English into France. His son Philip, the new Duke of Burgundy, viewing the dauphin as guilty of his death, went over with all his forces to Henry V., taking with him the queen and the poor helpless king. At the treaty of Troyes, in 1420, Henry was declared regent, and heir of the kingdom, at the same time as he received the hand of Catherine, daughter of Charles VI. This gave him Paris and all the chief cities in northern France; but the Armagnacs held the south, with the Dauphin Charles at their head. Charles was declared an outlaw by his father's court, but he was in truth the leader of what had become the national and patriotic cause. During this time, after a long struggle and schism, the Pope again returned to Rome.

11. The Maid of Orleans. — When Henry V. died in 1422, and the unhappy Charles a few weeks later, the infant Henry VI. was proclaimed King of France as well as of England, at both Paris and London, while *Charles VII.* was only proclaimed at Bourges, and a few other places in the south. Charles was of a slow, sluggish nature, and the men around him were selfish and pleasure-loving intriguers, who kept aloof all the bolder spirits from him. The brother of Henry V., John, Duke of Bedford, ruled all the country north of

the Loire, with Rouen as his head-quarters. For seven years little was done; but in 1429 he caused Orleans to be besieged. The city held out bravely, all France looked on anxiously, and a young peasant girl, named Joan d'Arc, believed herself called by voices from the saints to rescue the city, and lead the king to his coronation at Rheims. With difficulty she obtained a hearing of the king, and was allowed to proceed to Orleans. Leading the army with a consecrated sword, which she never stained with blood, she filled the French with confidence, the English with fear as of a witch, and thus she gained the day wherever she appeared. Orleans was saved, and she then conducted Charles VII. to Rheims, and stood beside his throne when he was crowned. Then she said her work was done, and would have returned home; but, though the wretched king and his court never appreciated her, they thought her useful with the soldiers, and would not let her leave them. She had lost her heart and hope, and the men began to be angered at her for putting down all vice and foul language. The captains were envious of her; and at last, when she had led a sally out of the besieged town of Compiègne, the gates were shut, and she was made prisoner by a Burgundian, John of Luxembourg. The Burgundians hated her even more than the English. The inquisitor was of their party, and a court was held at Rouen, which condemned her to die as a witch. Bedford consented, but left the city before the execution. Her own king made no effort to save her, though, many years later, he caused enquiries to be made, established her innocence, ennobled her family, and freed her village from taxation.

12. Recovery of France (1434 — 1450). — But though Joan was gone, her work lasted. The Constable, Artur of Richmond, the Count of Dunois, and

other brave leaders, continued to attack the English. After seventeen years' vengeance for his father's death, the Duke of Burgundy made his peace with Charles by a treaty at Arras, on condition of paying no more homage, in 1434. Bedford died soon after, and there were nothing but disputes among the English. Paris opened its gates to the king, and Charles, almost in spite of himself, was restored. An able merchant, named Jacques Cœur, lent him money which equipped his men for the recovery of Normandy, and he himself, waking into activity, took Rouen and the other cities on the coast.

13. Conquest of Aquitaine (1450). — By these successes Charles had recovered all, save Calais, that Henry V. or Edward III. had taken from France. But he was now able to do more. The one province of the south which the French kings had never been able to win was Guienne, the duchy on the river Garonne. Guienne had been a part of Eleanor's inheritance, and passed through her to the English kings; but though they had lost all else, the hatred of its inhabitants to the French enabled them to retain this, and Guienne had never yet passed under French rule. It was wrested, however, from Eleanor's descendants in this flood-tide of conquest. Bordeaux held out as long as it could, but Henry VI. could send no aid, and it was forced to yield. Two years later, brave old Lord Talbot led 5000 men to recover the duchy, and was gladly welcomed; but he was slain in the battle of Castillon, fighting like a lion. His two sons fell beside him, and his army was broken. Bordeaux again surrendered, and the French kings at last found themselves master of the great fief of the south. Calais was, at the close of the great Hundred Years' War, the only possession left to England south of the Channel.

14. The Standing Army (1452). — As at the end of the first act in the Hundred Years' War, the great difficulty in time of peace was the presence of the bands of free companions, or mercenary soldiers, who, when war and plunder failed them, lived by violence and robbery of the peasants. Charles VII., who had awakened into vigour, thereupon took into regular pay all who would submit to discipline, and the rest were led off on two futile expeditions into Switzerland and Germany, and there left to their fate. The princes and nobles were at first so much disgusted at the regulations which bound the soldiery to respect the magistracy, that they raised a rebellion, which was fostered by the Dauphin Louis, who was ready to do anything that could annoy his father. But he was soon detached from them; the Duke of Burgundy would not assist them, and the league fell to pieces. Charles VII. by thus retaining companies of hired troops in his pay laid the foundation of the first standing army in Europe, and enabled the monarchy to tread down the feudal force of the nobles. His government was firm and wise; and with his reign began better times for France. But it was long before it recovered from the miseries of the long strife. The war had kept back much of progress. There had been grievous havoc of buildings in the north and centre of France; much lawlessness and cruelty prevailed; and yet there was a certain advance in learning, and much love of romance and the theory of chivalry. Pages of noble birth were bred up in castles to be first squires and then knights. There was immense formality and stateliness, the order of precedence was most minute, and pomp and display were wonderful. Strange alternations took place. One month the streets of Paris would be a scene of horrible famine, where hungry dogs, and even wolves, put an end to the miseries of starving,

homeless children of slaughtered parents; another, the people would be gazing at royal banquets, lasting a whole day, with allegorical "subtleties" of jelly on the table, and pageants coming between the courses, where all the Virtues harangued in turn, or where knights delivered maidens from giants and "salvage men." In the south there was less misery and more progress. Jacques Cœur's house at Bourges is still a marvel of household architecture; and René, Duke of Anjou and Count of Provence, was an excellent painter on glass, and also a poet.

CHAPTER III.

THE STRUGGLE WITH BURGUNDY.

1. Power of Burgundy. — All the troubles of France, for the last 80 years, had gone to increase the strength of the Dukes of Burgundy. The county and duchy, of which Dijon was the capital, lay in the most fertile district of France, and had, as we have seen, been conferred on Philip the Bold. His marriage had given to him Flanders, with a gallant nobility, and with the chief manufacturing cities of Northern Europe. Philip's son, John the Fearless, had married a lady who ultimately brought into the family the great imperial counties of Holland and Zealand; and her son, Duke Philip the Good, by purchase or inheritance, obtained possession of all the adjoining little fiefs forming the country called the Netherlands, some belonging to the Empire, some to France. Philip had turned the scale in the struggle between England and France, and, as his reward, had won the cities on the Somme. He had thus become the richest and most powerful prince in Europe, and seemed on the point of founding a middle state lying between France and Germany, his weak point being that the imperial fiefs in Lorraine and Elsass lay between his dukedom of Burgundy and his counties in the Netherlands. No European court equalled in splendour that of Philip. The great cities of Ghent, Bruges, Antwerp, and the rest, though full of fierce and resolute men, paid him dues enough to make him the richest of princes, and the Flemish knights were among the boldest in Europe. All the arts of life, above all painting and domestic architecture, nourished at Brussels; and nowhere were troops so well equipped, burghers more prosperous, learning more widespread, than in his

domains. Here, too, were the most ceremonious courtesy, the most splendid banquets, and the most wonderful display of jewels, plate, and cloth-of-gold. Charles VII., a clever though a cold-hearted, indolent man, let Philip alone, already seeing how the game would go for the future; for when the dauphin had quarrelled with the reigning favourite, and was kindly received on his flight to Burgundy, the old king sneered, saying that the duke was fostering the fox who would steal his chickens.

2. Louis XI.'s Policy. — *Louis XI.* succeeded his father Charles in 1461. He was a man of great skill and craft, with an iron will, and subtle though pitiless nature, who knew in what the greatness of a king consisted, and worked out his ends mercilessly and unscrupulously. The old feudal dukes and counts had all passed away, except the Duke of Brittany; but the Dukes of Orleans, Burgundy, and Anjou held princely appanages, and there was a turbulent nobility who had grown up during the wars, foreign and civil, and been encouraged by the favouritism of Charles VI. All these, feeling that Louis was their natural foe, united against him in what was called the "League of the Public Good," with his own brother, the Duke of Berry, and Count Charles of Charolais, who was known as Charles the Bold, the son of Duke Philip of Burgundy, at their head. Louis was actually defeated by Charles of Charolais in the battle of Montlhéry; but he contrived so cleverly to break up the league, by promises to each member and by sowing dissension among them, that he ended by becoming more powerful than before.

3. Charles the Bold. — On the death of Philip the Good, in 1467, Charles the Bold succeeded to the duchy of Burgundy. He pursued more ardently the

plan of forming a new kingdom of Burgundy, and had even hopes of being chosen Emperor. First, however, he had to consolidate his dominions, by making himself master of the countries which parted Burgundy from the Netherlands. With this view he obtained Elsass in pledge from its owner, a needy son of the house of Austria, who was never likely to redeem it. Lorraine had been inherited by Yolande, the wife of René, Duke of Anjou and titular King of Sicily, and had passed from her to her daughter, who had married the nearest heir in the male line, the Count of Vaudémont; but Charles the Bold unjustly seized the dukedom, driving out the lawful heir, René de Vaudémont, son of this marriage. Louis, meantime, was on the watch for every error of Charles, and constantly sowing dangers in his path. Sometimes his mines exploded too soon, as when he had actually put himself into Charles's power by visiting him at Peronne at the very moment when his emissaries had encouraged the city of Liège to rise in revolt against their bishop, an ally of the duke; and he only bought his freedom by profuse promises, and by aiding Charles in a most savage destruction of Liège. But after this his caution prevailed. He gave secret support to the adherents of René de Vaudémont, and intrigued with the Swiss, who were often at issue with the Burgundian bailiffs and soldiery in Elsass — greedy, reckless men, from whom the men of Elsass revolted in favour of their former Austrian lord. Meantime Edward IV. of England, Charles's brother-in-law, had planned with him an invasion of France and division of the kingdom, and in 1475 actually crossed the sea with a splendid host; but while Charles was prevented from joining him by the siege of Neuss, a city in alliance with Sigismund of Austria, Louis met Edward on the bridge of Pecquigny, and by cajolery, bribery, and accusations of Charles, contrived to persuade him to carry home his army without striking a blow. That meeting was a curious one. A wooden barrier, like a wild beast's cage, was erected in the middle of the bridge, through which the two kings kissed one another. Edward was the tallest and handsomest man present, and splendidly attired. Louis was small and mean-looking, and clad in an old blue suit, with a hat decorated with little leaden images of the saints, but his smooth tongue quite overcame the duller intellect of Edward; and in the mean time the English soldiers were feasted and allowed their full swing, the French being strictly watched to prevent all quarrels. So skilfully did Louis manage, that Edward consented to make peace and return home.

4. The Fall of Charles the Bold (1477). — Charles had become entangled in many difficulties. He was a harsh, stern man, much disliked; and his governors in Elsass were fierce, violent men, who used every pretext for preying upon travellers. The Governor of Breisach, Hagenbach, had been put to death in a popular rising, aided by the Swiss of Berne, in 1474; and the men of Elsass themselves raised part of the sum for which the country had been pledged, and revolted against Charles. The Swiss were incited by Louis to join them; René of Lorraine made common cause with them. In two great battles, Granson and Morat, Charles and all his chivalry were beaten by the Swiss pikemen; but he pushed on the war. Nancy, the chief city of Lorraine, had risen against him, and he besieged it. On the night of the 5th of January, 1477, René led the Swiss to relieve the town by falling in early morning on the besiegers' camp. There was a terrible fight; the Burgundians were routed, and after long search the corpse of Duke Charles was found in a frozen pool, stripped, plundered, and covered with

blood. He was the last of the male line of Burgundy, and its great possessions broke up with his death. His only child, Marie, did not inherit the French dukedom nor the county, though most of the fiefs in the Low Countries, which could descend to the female line, were her undisputed portion. Louis tried, by stirring up her subjects, to force her into a marriage with his son Charles; but she threw herself on the protection of the house of Austria, and marrying Maximilian, son of the Emperor Frederick III., carried her border lands to swell the power of his family.

5. Louis's Home Government. — Louis's system of repression of the nobles went on all this time. His counsellors were of low birth (Oliver le Daim, his barber, was the man he most trusted), his habits frugal, his manners reserved and ironical; he was dreaded, hated, and distrusted, and he became constantly more bitter, suspicious, and merciless. Those who fell under his displeasure were imprisoned in iron cages, or put to death; and the more turbulent families, such as the house of Armagnac, were treated with frightful severity. But his was not wanton violence. He acted on a regular system of depressing the lawless nobility and increasing the royal authority, by bringing the power of the cities forward, by trusting for protection to the standing army, chiefly of hired Scots, Swiss, and Italians, and by saving money. By this means he was able to purchase the counties of Roussillon and Perpignan from the King of Aragon, thus making the Pyrenees his frontier, and on several occasions he made his treasury fight his battles instead of the swords of his knights. He lived in the castle of Plessis les Tours, guarded by the utmost art of fortification, and filled with hired Scottish archers of his guard, whom he preferred as defenders to his own nobles. He was exceedingly unpopular with his

nobles; but the statesman and historian, Philip de Comines, who had gone over to him from Charles of Burgundy, viewed him as the best and ablest of kings. He did much to promote trade and manufacture, improved the cities, fostered the university, and was in truth the first king since Philip Augustus who had any real sense of statesmanship. But though the burghers throve under him, and the lawless nobles were depressed, the state of the peasants was not improved; feudal rights pressed heavily on them, and they were little better than savages, ground down by burthens imposed by their lords.

6. Provence and Brittany. — Louis had added much to the French monarchy. He had won back Artois; he had seized the duchy and county of Burgundy; he had bought Roussillon. His last acquisition was the county of Provence. The second Angevin family, beginning with Louis, the son of King John, had never succeeded in gaining a footing in Naples, though they bore the royal title. They held, however, the imperial fief of Provence, and Louis XI., whose mother had been of this family, obtained from her two brothers, René and Charles, that Provence should be bequeathed to him instead of passing to René's grandson, the Duke of Lorraine. The Kings of France were thenceforth Counts of Provence; and though the county was not viewed as part of the kingdom, it was practically one with it. A yet greater acquisition was made soon after Louis's death in 1483. The great Celtic duchy of Brittany fell to a female, Anne of Brittany, and the address of Louis's daughter, the Lady of Beaujeu, who was regent of the realm, prevailed to secure the hand of the heiress for her brother, Charles VIII. Thus the crown of France had by purchase, conquest, or inheritance, obtained all the great feudal states that made up the country between the English

Channel and the Pyrenees; but each still remained a separate state, with different laws and customs, and a separate parliament in each to register laws, and to act as a court of justice.

CHAPTER IV.

THE ITALIAN WARS.

1. Campaign of Charles VIII. (1493). — From grasping at province after province on their own border, however, the French kings were now to turn to wider dreams of conquest abroad. Together with the county of Provence, Louis XI. had bought from King René all the claims of the house of Anjou. Among these was included a claim to the kingdom of Naples. Louis's son, *Charles VIII.*, a vain and shallow lad, was tempted by the possession of large treasures and a fine army to listen to the persuasions of an Italian intriguer, Ludovico Sforza, Duke of Milan, and put forward these pretensions, thus beginning a war which lasted nearly as long as the Hundred Years' War with England. But it was a war of aggression instead of a war of self-defence. Charles crossed the Alps in 1493, marched the whole length of Italy without opposition, and was crowned at Naples; while its royal family, an illegitimate offshoot from the Kings of Aragon, fled into Sicily, and called on Spain for help. But the insolent exactions of the French soldiery caused the people to rise against them; and when Charles returned, he was beset at Fornovo by a great league of Italians, over whom he gained a complete victory. Small and puny though he was, he fought like a lion, and seemed quite inspired by the ardour of combat. The "French fury," *la furia Francese*, became a proverb among the Italians. Charles neglected, however, to send any supplies or reinforcements to the garrisons he had left behind him in Naples, and they all perished under want, sickness, and the sword of the Spaniards. He was meditating another expedition, when he struck his head against the top of a doorway,

and died in 1498.

2. Campaign of Louis XII. — His cousin, *Louis XII.*, married his widow, and thus prevented Brittany from again parting from the crown. Louis not only succeeded to the Angevin right to Naples, but through his grandmother he viewed himself as heir of Milan. She was Valentina Visconti, wife to that Duke of Orleans who had been murdered by John the Fearless. Louis himself never advanced further than to Milan, whose surrender made him master of Lombardy, which he held for the greater part of his reign. But after a while the Spanish king, Ferdinand, agreed with him to throw over the cause of the unfortunate royal family of Naples, and divide that kingdom between them. Louis XII. sent a brilliant army to take possession of his share, but the bounds of each portion had not been defined, and the French and Spanish troops began a war even while their kings were still treating with one another. The individual French knights did brilliant exploits, for indeed it was the time of the chief blossom of fanciful chivalry, a knight of Dauphiné, named Bayard, called the Fearless and Stainless Knight, and honoured by friend and foe; but the Spaniards were under Gonzalo de Cordova, called the Great Captain, and after the battles of Cerignola and the Garigliano drove the French out of the kingdom of Naples, though the war continued in Lombardy.

3. The Holy League. — It was an age of leagues. The Italians, hating French and Spaniards both alike, were continually forming combinations among themselves and with foreign powers against whichever happened to be the strongest. The chief of these was called the Holy League, because it was formed by Pope Julius II., who drew into it Maximilian, then

head of the German Empire, Ferdinand of Spain, and Henry VIII. of England. The French troops were attacked in Milan; and though they gained the battle of Ravenna in 1512, it was with the loss of their general, Gaston de Foix, Duke of Nemours, whose death served as an excuse to Ferdinand of Spain for setting up a claim to the kingdom of Navarre. He cunningly persuaded Henry VIII. to aid him in the attack, by holding out the vain idea of going on to regain Gascony; and while one troop of English were attacking Pampeluna, Henry himself landed at Calais and took Tournay and Terouenne. The French forces were at the same time being chased out of Italy. However, when Pampeluna had been taken, and the French finally driven out of Lombardy, the Pope and king, who had gained their ends, left Henry to fight his own battles. He thus was induced to make peace, giving his young sister Mary as second wife to Louis; but that king over-exerted himself at the banquets, and died six weeks after the marriage, in 1515. During this reign the waste of blood and treasure on wars of mere ambition was frightful, and the country had been heavily taxed; but a brilliant soldiery had been trained up, and national vanity had much increased. The king, though without deserving much love, was so kindly in manner that he was a favourite, and was called the Father of the People. His first wife, Anne of Brittany, was an excellent and high-spirited woman, who kept the court of France in a better state than ever before or since.

4. Campaigns of Francis I. — Louis left only two daughters, the elder of whom, Claude, carried Brittany to his male heir, Francis, Count of Angoulêine. Anne of Brittany had been much averse to the match; but Louis said he kept his mice for his own cats, and gave his daughter and her duchy to Francis as soon as

Anne was dead. *Francis I.* was one of the vainest, falsest, and most dashing of Frenchmen. In fact, he was an exaggeration in every way of the national character, and thus became a national hero, much overpraised. He at once resolved to recover Lombardy; and after crossing the Alps encountered an army of Swiss troops, who had been hired to defend the Milanese duchy, on the field of Marignano. Francis had to fight a desperate battle with them; after which he caused Bayard to dub him knight, though French kings were said to be born knights. In gaining the victory over these mercenaries, who had been hitherto deemed invincible, he opened for himself a way into Italy, and had all Lombardy at his feet. The Pope, Leo X., met him at Bologna, and a concordat took place, by which the French Church became more entirely subject to the Pope, while in return all patronage was given up to the crown. The effects were soon seen in the increased corruption of the clergy and people. Francis brought home from this expedition much taste for Italian art and literature, and all matters of elegance and ornament made great progress from this time. The great Italian masters worked for him; Raphael painted some of his most beautiful pictures for him, and Leonardo da Vinci came to his court, and there died in his arms. His palaces, especially that of Blois, were exceedingly beautiful, in the new classic style, called the Renaissance. Great richness and splendour reigned at court, and set off his pretensions to romance and chivalry. Learning and scholarship, especially classical, increased much; and the king's sister, Margaret, Queen of Navarre, was an excellent and highly cultivated woman, but even her writings prove that the whole tone of feeling was terribly coarse, when not vicious.

5. Charles V. — The conquest of Lombardy made

France the greatest power in Christendom; but its king was soon to find a mighty and active rival. The old hatred between France and Burgundy again awoke. Mary of Burgundy, the daughter of Charles the Bold, had married Maximilian, Archduke of Austria and King of the Romans, though never actually crowned Emperor. Their son, Philip, married Juana, the daughter of Ferdinand, and heiress of Spain, who lost her senses from grief on Philip's untimely death; and thus the direct heir to Spain, Austria, and the Netherlands, was Charles, her eldest son. On the death of Maximilian in 1518, Francis proposed himself to the electors as Emperor, but failed, in spite of bribery. Charles was chosen, and from that time Francis pursued him with unceasing hatred. The claims to Milan and Naples were renewed. Francis sent troops to occupy Milan, and was following them himself; but the most powerful of all his nobles, the Duke of Bourbon, Constable of France, had been alienated by an injustice perpetrated on him in favour of the king's mother, and deserted to the Spaniards, offering to assist them and the English in dividing France, while he reserved for himself Provence. His desertion hindered Francis from sending support to the troops in Milan, who were forced to retreat. Bayard was shot in the spine while defending the rear-guard, and was left to die under a tree. The utmost honour was shown him by the Spaniards; but when Bourbon came near him, he bade him take pity, not on one who was dying as a true soldier, but on himself as a traitor to king and country. When the French, in 1525, invaded Lombardy, Francis suffered a terrible defeat at Pavia, and was carried a prisoner to Madrid, where he remained for a year, and was only set free on making a treaty by which he was to give up all claims in Italy both to Naples and Milan, also the county of Burgundy and the suzerainty of those Flemish counties which had been fiefs of the French crown, as well as to surrender his two sons as hostages for the performance of the conditions.

6. Wars of Francis and Charles. — All the rest of the king's life was an attempt to elude or break these conditions, against which he had protested in his prison, but when there was no Spaniard present to hear him do so. The county of Burgundy refused to be transferred; and the Pope, Clement VII., hating the Spanish power in Italy, contrived a fresh league against Charles, in which Francis joined, but was justly rewarded by the miserable loss of another army. His mother and Charles's aunt met at Cambrai, and concluded, in 1529, what was called the Ladies' Peace, which bore as hardly on France as the peace of Madrid, excepting that Charles gave up his claim to Burgundy. Still Francis's plans were not at an end. He married his second son, Henry, to Catherine, the only legitimate child of the great Florentine house of Medici, and tried to induce Charles to set up an Italian dukedom of Milan for the young pair; but when the dauphin died, and Henry became heir of France, Charles would not give him any footing in Italy. Francis never let any occasion pass of harassing the Emperor, but was always defeated. Charles once actually invaded Provence, but was forced to retreat through the devastation of the country before him by Montmorençy, afterwards Constable of France. Francis, by loud complaints, and by talking much of his honour, contrived to make the world fancy him the injured man, while he was really breaking oaths in a shameless manner. At last, in 1537, the king and Emperor met at Aigues Mortes, and came to terms. Francis married, as his second wife, Charles's sister Eleanor, and in 1540, when Charles was in haste to quell a re-

volt in the Low Countries, he asked a safe conduct through France, and was splendidly entertained at Paris. Yet so low was the honour of the French, that Francis scarcely withstood the temptation of extorting the duchy of Milan from him when in his power, and gave so many broad hints that Charles was glad to be past the frontier. The war was soon renewed. Francis set up a claim to Savoy, as the key of Italy, allied himself with the Turks and Moors, and slaves taken by them on the coasts of Italy and Spain were actually brought into Marseilles. Nice was burnt; but the citadel held out, and as Henry VIII. had allied himself with the Emperor, and had taken Boulogne, Francis made a final peace at Crespy in 1545. He died only two years later, in 1547.

7. Henry II. — His only surviving son, *Henry II.*, followed the same policy. The rise of Protestantism was now dividing the Empire in Germany; and Henry took advantage of the strife which broke out between Charles and the Protestant princes to attack the Emperor, and make conquests across the German border. He called himself Protector of the Liberties of the Germans, and leagued himself with them, seizing Metz, which the Duke of Guise bravely defended when the Emperor tried to retake it. This seizure of Metz was the first attempt of France to make conquests in Germany, and the beginning of a contest between the French and German peoples which has gone on to the present day. After the siege a five years' truce was made, during which Charles V. resigned his crowns. His brother had been already elected to the Empire, but his son Philip II. became King of Spain and Naples, and also inherited the Low Countries. The Pope, Paul IV., who was a Neapolitan, and hated the Spanish rule, incited Henry, a vain, weak man, to break the truce and send one army to

Italy, under the Duke of Guise, while another attacked the frontier of the Netherlands. Philip, assisted by the forces of his wife, Mary I. of England, met this last attack with an army commanded by the Duke of Savoy. It advanced into France, and besieged St. Quentin. The French, under the Constable of Montmorençy, came to relieve the city, and were utterly defeated, the Constable himself being made prisoner. His nephew, the Admiral de Coligny, held out St. Quentin to the last, and thus gave the country time to rally against the invader; and Guise was recalled in haste from Italy. He soon after surprised Calais, which was thus restored to the French, after having been held by the English for two hundred years. This was the only conquest the French retained when the final peace of Cateau Cambresis was made in the year 1558, for all else that had been taken on either side was then restored. Savoy was given back to its duke, together with the hand of Henry's sister, Margaret. During a tournament held in honour of the wedding, Henry II. was mortally injured by the splinter of a lance, in 1559; and in the home troubles that followed, all pretensions to Italian power were dropped by France, after wars which had lasted sixty-four years.

CHAPTER V.

THE WARS OF RELIGION.

1. The Bourbons and Guises. — Henry II. had left four sons, the eldest of whom, *Francis II.*, was only fifteen years old; and the country was divided by two great factions — one headed by the Guise family, an offshoot of the house of Lorraine; the other by the Bourbons, who, being descended in a direct male line from a younger son of St. Louis, were the next heirs to the throne in case the house of Valois should become extinct. Antony, the head of the Bourbon family, was called King of Navarre, because of his marriage with Jeanne d'Albrêt, the queen, in her own right, of this Pyrenean kingdom, which was in fact entirely in the hands of the Spaniards, so that her only actual possession consisted of the little French counties of Foix and Béarn. Antony himself was dull and indolent, but his wife was a woman of much ability; and his brother, Louis, Prince of Condé, was full of spirit and fire, and little inclined to brook the ascendancy which the Duke of Guise and his brothers enjoyed at court, partly in consequence of his exploit at Calais, and partly from being uncle to the young Queen Mary of Scotland, wife of Francis II. The Bourbons likewise headed the party among the nobles who hoped to profit by the king's youth to recover the privileges of which they had been gradually deprived, while the house of Guise were ready to maintain the power of the crown, as long as that meant their own power.

2. The Reformation. — The enmity of these two parties was much increased by the reaction against the prevalent doctrines and the corruptions of the clergy. This reaction had begun in the reign of Francis I., when the Bible had been translated into French by

two students at the University of Paris, and the king's sister, Margaret, Queen of Navarre, had encouraged the Reformers. Francis had leagued with the German Protestants because they were foes to the Emperor, while he persecuted the like opinions at home to satisfy the Pope. John Calvin, a native of Picardy, the foremost French reformer, was invited to the free city of Geneva, and there was made chief pastor, while the scheme of theology called his "Institutes" became the text-book of the Reformed in France, Scotland, and Holland. His doctrine was harsh and stern, aiming at the utmost simplicity of worship, and denouncing the existing practices so fiercely, that the people, who held themselves to have been wilfully led astray by their clergy, committed such violence in the churches that the Catholics loudly called for punishment on them. The shameful lives of many of the clergy and the wickedness of the Court had caused a strong reaction against them, and great numbers of both nobles and burghers became Calvinists. They termed themselves Sacramentarians or Reformers, but their nickname was Huguenots; probably from the Swiss, "*Eidgenossen*" or oath comrades. Henry II., like his father, protected German Lutherans and persecuted French Calvinists; but the lawyers of the Parliament of Paris interposed, declaring that men ought not to be burnt for heresy until a council of the Church should have condemned their opinions, and it was in the midst of this dispute that Henry was slain.

3. The Conspiracy of Amboise. — The Guise family were strong Catholics; the Bourbons were the heads of the Huguenot party, chiefly from policy; but Admiral Coligny and his brother, the Sieur D'Andelot, were sincere and earnest Reformers. A third party, headed by the old Constable De Montmorençy, was Catholic in faith, but not unwilling to join with the

Huguenots in pulling down the Guises, and asserting the power of the nobility. A conspiracy for seizing the person of the king and destroying the Guises at the castle of Amboise was detected in time to make it fruitless. The two Bourbon princes kept in the background, though Condé was universally known to have been the true head and mover in it, and he was actually brought to trial. The discovery only strengthened the hands of Guise.

4. Regency of Catherine de' Medici. — Even then, however, Francis II. was dying, and his brother, *Charles IX.*, who succeeded him in 1560, was but ten years old. The regency passed to his mother, the Florentine Catherine, a wily, cat-like woman, who had always hitherto been kept in the background, and whose chief desire was to keep things quiet by playing off one party against the other. She at once released Condé, and favoured the Bourbons and the Huguenots to keep down the Guises, even permitting conferences to see whether the French Church could be reformed so as to satisfy the Calvinists. Proposals were sent by Guise's brother, the Cardinal of Lorraine, to the council then sitting at Trent, for vernacular services, the marriage of the clergy, and other alterations which might win back the Reformers. But an attack by the followers of Guise on a meeting of Calvinists at Vassy, of whose ringing of bells his mother had complained, led to the first bloodshed and the outbreak of a civil war.

5. The Religious War. — To trace each stage of the war would be impossible within these limits. It was a war often lulled for a short time, and often breaking out again, and in which the actors grew more and more cruel. The Reformed influence was in the south, the Catholic in the east. Most of the provin-

cial cities at first held with the Bourbons, for the sake of civil and religious freedom; though the Guise family succeeded to the popularity of the Burgundian dukes in Paris. Still Catherine persuaded Antony of Bourbon to return to court just as his wife, Queen Jeanne of Navarre, had become a staunch Calvinist, and while dreaming of exchanging his claim on Navarre for the kingdom of Sardinia, he was killed on the Catholic side while besieging Rouen. At the first outbreak the Huguenots seemed to have by far the greatest influence. An endeavour was made to seize the king's person, and this led to a battle at Dreux. While it was doubtful Catherine actually declared, "We shall have to say our prayers in French." Guise, however, retrieved the day, and though Montmorençy was made prisoner on the one side, Condé was taken on the other. Orleans was the Huguenot rallying-place, and while besieging it Guise himself was assassinated. His death was believed by his family to be due to the Admiral de Coligny. The city of Rochelle, fortified by Jeanne of Navarre, became the stronghold of the Huguenots. Leader after leader fell — Montmorençy, on the one hand, was killed at Montcontour; Condé, on the other, was shot in cold blood after the fight of Jarnac. A truce followed, but was soon broken again, and in 1571 Coligny was the only man of age and standing at the head of the Huguenot party; while the Catholics had as leaders Henry, Duke of Anjou, the king's brother, and Henry, Duke of Guise, both young men of little more than twenty. The Huguenots had been beaten at all points, but were still strong enough to have wrung from their enemies permission to hold meetings for public worship within unwalled towns and on the estates of such nobles as held with them.

      6. Catherine's Policy. — Catherine made use of

the suspension of arms to try to detach the Huguenot leaders, by entangling them in the pleasures of the court and lowering their sense of duty. The court was studiously brilliant. Catherine surrounded herself with a bevy of ladies, called the Queen-Mother's Squadron, whose amusements were found for the whole day. The ladies sat at their tapestry frames, while Italian poetry and romance was read or love-songs sung by the gentlemen; they had garden games and hunting-parties, with every opening for the ladies to act as sirens to any whom the queen wished to detach from the principles of honour and virtue, and bind to her service. Balls, pageants, and theatricals followed in the evening, and there was hardly a prince or noble in France who was not carried away by these seductions into darker habits of profligacy. Jeanne of Navarre dreaded them for her son Henry, whom she kept as long as possible under training in religion, learning, and hardy habits, in the mountains of Béarn; and when Catherine tried to draw him to court by proposing a marriage between him and her youngest daughter Margaret, Jeanne left him at home, and went herself to court. Catherine tried in vain to bend her will or discover her secrets, and her death, early in 1572, while still at court, was attributed to the queen-mother.

7. Massacre of St. Bartholomew (1572). — Jeanne's son Henry was immediately summoned to conclude the marriage, and came attended by all the most distinguished Huguenots, though the more wary of them remained at home, and the Baron of Rosny said, "If that wedding takes place the favours will be crimson." The Duke of Guise seems to have resolved on taking this opportunity of revenging himself for his father's murder, but the queen-mother was undecided until she found that her son Charles, who

had been bidden to cajole and talk over the Huguenot chiefs, had been attracted by their honesty and uprightness, and was ready to throw himself into their hands, and escape from hers. An abortive attempt on Guise's part to murder the Admiral Coligny led to all the Huguenots going about armed, and making demonstrations which alarmed both the queen and the people of Paris. Guise and the Duke of Anjou were, therefore, allowed to work their will, and to rouse the bloodthirstiness of the Paris mob. At midnight of the 24th of August, 1572, St. Bartholomew's night, the bell of the church of St. Germain l'Auxerrois began to ring, and the slaughter was begun by men distinguished by a white sleeve. The king sheltered his Huguenot surgeon and nurse in his room. The young King of Navarre and Prince of Condé were threatened into conforming to the Church, but every other Huguenot who could be found was massacred, from Coligny, who was slain kneeling in his bedroom by the followers of Guise, down to the poorest and youngest, and the streets resounded with the cry, "Kill! kill!" In every city where royal troops and Guisard partisans had been living among Huguenots, the same hideous work took place for three days, sparing neither age nor sex. How many thousands died, it is impossible to reckon, but the work was so wholesale that none were left except those in the southern cities, where the Huguenots had been too strong to be attacked, and in those castles where the seigneur was of "the religion." The Catholic party thought the destruction complete, the court went in state to return thanks for deliverance from a supposed plot, while Coligny's body was hung on a gibbet. The Pope ordered public thanksgivings, while Queen Elizabeth put on mourning, and the Emperor Maximilian II., alone among Catholic princes, showed any horror or indignation. But the heart of the unhappy young king was broken by the guilt he had incurred. Charles IX. sank into a decline, and died in 1574, finding no comfort save in the surgeon and nurse he had saved.

8. The League. — His brother, *Henry III.*, who had been elected King of Poland, threw up that crown in favour of that of France. He was of a vain, false, weak character, superstitiously devout, and at the same time ferocious, so as to alienate every one. All were ashamed of a man who dressed in the extreme of foppery, with a rosary of death's heads at his girdle, and passed from wild dissipation to abject penance. He was called "the Paris Church-warden and the Queen's Hairdresser," for he passed from her toilette to the decoration of the walls of churches with illuminations cut out of old service-books. Sometimes he went about surrounded with little dogs, sometimes flogged himself walking barefoot in a procession, and his *mignons*, or favourites, were the scandal of the country by their pride, license, and savage deeds. The war broke out again, and his only remaining brother, Francis, Duke of Alençon, an equally hateful and contemptible being, fled from court to the Huguenot army, hoping to force his brother into buying his submission; but when the King of Navarre had followed him and begun the struggle in earnest, he accepted the duchy of Anjou, and returned to his allegiance. Francis was invited by the insurgent Dutch to become their chief, and spent some time in Holland, but returned, unsuccessful and dying. As the king was childless, the next male heir was Henry of Bourbon, King of Navarre, who had fled from court soon after Alençon returned to the Huguenot faith, and was reigning in his two counties of Béarn and Foix, the head of the Huguenots. In the resolve never to permit a heretic to wear the French crown, Guise and

his party formed a Catholic league, to force Henry III. to choose another successor. Paris was devoted to Guise, and the king, finding himself almost a prisoner there, left the city, but was again mastered by the duke at Blois, and could so ill brook his arrogance, as to have recourse to assassination. He caused him to be slain at the palace at Blois in 1588. The fury of the League was so great that Henry III. was driven to take refuge with the King of Navarre, and they were together besieging Paris, when Henry III. was in his turn murdered by a monk, named Clement, in 1589.

9. Henry IV. — The Leaguers proclaimed as king an old uncle of the King of Navarre, the Cardinal of Bourbon, but all the more moderate Catholics rallied round Henry of Navarre, who took the title of *Henry IV*. At Ivry, in Normandy, Henry met the force of Leaguers, and defeated them by his brilliant courage. "Follow my white plume," his last order to his troops, became one of the sayings the French love to remember. But his cause was still not won — Paris held out against him, animated by almost fanatical fury, and while he was besieging it France was invaded from the Netherlands. The old Cardinal of Bourbon was now dead, and Philip II. considered his daughter Isabel, whose mother was the eldest daughter of Henry II., to be rightful Queen of France. He sent therefore his ablest general, the Duke of Parma, to co-operate with the Leaguers and place her on the throne. A war of strategy was carried on, during which Henry kept the enemy at bay, but could do no more, since the larger number of his people, though intending to have no king but himself, did not wish him to gain too easy a victory, lest in that case he should remain a Calvinist. However, he was only waiting to recant till he could do so with a good grace. He really preferred Catholicism, and had only been a political Huguenot;

and his best and most faithful adviser, the Baron of Rosny, better known as Duke of Sully, though a staunch Calvinist himself, recommended the change as the only means of restoring peace to the kingdom. There was little more resistance to Henry after he had again been received by the Church in 1592. Paris, weary of the long war, opened its gates in 1593, and the inhabitants crowded round him with ecstasy, so that he said, "Poor people, they are hungry for the sight of a king!" The Leaguers made their peace, and when Philip of Spain again attacked Henry, the young Duke of Guise was one of the first to hasten to the defence. Philip saw that there were no further hopes for his daughter, and peace was made in 1596.

10. The Edict of Nantes. — Two years later, in 1598, Henry put forth what was called the Edict of Nantes, because first registered in that parliament. It secured to the Huguenots equal civil rights with those of the Catholics, accepted their marriages, gave them, under restrictions, permission to meet for worship and for consultations, and granted them cities for the security of their rights, of which La Rochelle was the chief. The Calvinists had been nearly exterminated in the north, but there were still a large number in the south of France, and the burghers of the chief southern cities were mostly Huguenot. The war had been from the first a very horrible one; there had been savage slaughter, and still more savage reprisals on each side. The young nobles had been trained into making a fashion of ferocity, and practising graceful ways of striking death-blows. Whole districts had been laid waste, churches and abbeys destroyed, tombs rifled, and the whole population accustomed to every sort of horror and suffering; while nobody but Henry IV. himself, and the Duke of Sully, had any notion either of statesmanship or of religious toleration.

11. Henry's Plans. — Just as the reign of Louis XI. had been a period of rest and recovery from the English wars, so that of Henry IV. was one of restoration from the ravages of thirty years of intermittent civil war. The king himself not only had bright and engaging manners, but was a man of large heart and mind; and Sully did much for the welfare of the country. Roads, canals, bridges, postal communications, manufactures, extended commerce, all owed their promotion to him, and brought prosperity to the burgher class; and the king was especially endeared to the peasantry by his saying that he hoped for the time when no cottage would be without a good fowl in its pot. The great silk manufactories of southern France chiefly arose under his encouragement, and there was prosperity of every kind. The Church itself was in a far better state than before. Some of the best men of any time were then living — in especial Vincent de Paul, who did much to improve the training of the parochial clergy, and who founded the order of Sisters of Charity, who prevented the misery of the streets of Paris from ever being so frightful as in those days when deserted children became the prey of wolves, dogs, and pigs. The nobles, who had grown into insolence during the wars, either as favourites of Henry III. or as zealous supporters of the Huguenot cause, were subdued and tamed. The most noted of these were the Duke of Bouillon, the owner of the small principality of Sedan, who was reduced to obedience by the sight of Sully's formidable train of artillery; and the Marshal Duke of Biron, who, thinking that Henry had not sufficiently rewarded his services, intrigued with Spain and Savoy, and was beheaded for his treason. Hatred to the house of Austria in Spain and Germany was as keen as ever in France; and in 1610 Henry IV. was prepared for another war

on the plea of a disputed succession to the duchy of Cleves. The old fanaticism still lingered in Paris, and Henry had been advised to beware of pageants there; but it was necessary that his second wife, Mary de' Medici, should be crowned before he went to the war, as she was to be left regent. Two days after the coronation, as Henry was going to the arsenal to visit his old friend Sully, he was stabbed to the heart in his coach, in the streets of Paris, by a fanatic named Ravaillac. The French call him Le Grand Monarque; and he was one of the most attractive and benevolent of men, winning the hearts of all who approached him, but the immorality of his life did much to confirm the already low standard that prevailed among princes and nobles in France.

12. The States-General of 1614. — Henry's second wife, Mary de' Medici, became regent, for her son, *Louis XIII.*, was only ten years old, and indeed his character was so weak that his whole reign was only one long minority. Mary de' Medici was entirely under the dominion of an Italian favourite named Concini, and his wife, and their whole endeavour was to amass riches for themselves and keep the young king in helpless ignorance, while they undid all that Sully had effected, and took bribes shamelessly. The Prince of Condé tried to overthrow them, and, in hopes of strengthening herself, in 1614 Mary summoned together the States-General. There came 464 members, 132 for the nobles, 140 for the clergy, and 192 for the third estate, *i.e.* the burghers, and these, being mostly lawyers and magistrates from the provinces, were resolved to make their voices heard. Taxation was growing worse and worse. Not only was it confined to the burgher and peasant class, exempting the clergy and the nobles, among which last were included their families to the remotest generation, but it had become

the court custom to multiply offices, in order to pension the nobles, and keep them quiet; and this, together with the expenses of the army, made the weight of taxation ruinous. Moreover, the presentation to the civil offices held by lawyers was made hereditary in their families, on payment of a sum down, and of fees at the death of each holder. All these abuses were complained of; and one of the deputies even told the nobility that if they did not learn to treat the despised classes below them as younger brothers, they would lay up a terrible store of retribution for themselves. A petition to the king was drawn up, and was received, but never answered. The doors of the house of assembly were closed — the members were told it was by order of the king — and the States-General never met again for 177 years, when the storm was just ready to fall.

13. The Siege of Rochelle. — The rottenness of the State was chiefly owing to the nobility, who, as long as they were allowed to grind down their peasants and shine at court, had no sense of duty or public spirit, and hated the burghers and lawyers far too much to make common cause with them against the constantly increasing power of the throne. They only intrigued and struggled for personal advantages and rivalries, and never thought of the good of the State. They bitterly hated Concini, the Marshal d'Ancre, as he had been created, but he remained in power till 1614, when one of the king's gentlemen, Albert de Luynes, plotted with the king himself and a few of his guards for his deliverance. Nothing could be easier than the execution. The king ordered the captain of the guards to arrest Concini, and kill him if he resisted; and this was done. Concini was cut down on the steps of the Louvre, and Louis exclaimed, "At last I am a king." But it was not in him to be a king, and he

never was one all his life. He only passed under the dominion of De Luynes, who was a high-spirited young noble. The Huguenots had been holding assemblies, which were considered more political than religious, and their towns of security were a grievance to royalty. War broke out again, and Louis himself went with De Luynes to besiege Montauban. The place was taken, but disease broke out in the army, and De Luynes died. There was a fresh struggle for power between the queen-mother and the Prince of Condé, ending in both being set aside by the queen's almoner, Armand de Richelieu, Bishop of Luçon, and afterwards a cardinal, the ablest statesman then in Europe, who gained complete dominion over the king and country, and ruled them both with a rod of iron. The Huguenots were gradually driven out of all their strongholds, till only Rochelle remained to them. This city was bravely and patiently defended by the magistrates and the Duke of Rohan, with hopes of succour from England, until these being disconcerted by the murder of the Duke of Buckingham, they were forced to surrender, after having held out for more than a year. Louis XIII. entered in triumph, deprived the city of all its privileges, and thus in 1628 concluded the war that had begun by the attack of the Guisards on the congregation at Vassy, in 1561. The lives and properties of the Huguenots were still secure, but all favour was closed against them, and every encouragement held out to them to join the Church. Many of the worst scandals had been removed, and the clergy were much improved; and, from whatever motive it might be, many of the more influential Huguenots began to conform to the State religion.

CHAPTER VI.

POWER OF THE CROWN.

1. Richelieu's Administration. — Cardinal de Richelieu's whole idea of statesmanship consisted in making the King of France the greatest of princes at home and abroad. To make anything great of Louis XIII., who was feeble alike in mind and body, was beyond any one's power, and Richelieu kept him in absolute subjection, allowing him a favourite with whom to hunt, talk, and amuse himself, but if the friend attempted to rouse the king to shake off the yoke, crushing him ruthlessly. It was the crown rather than the king that the cardinal exalted, putting down whatever resisted. Gaston, Duke of Orleans, the king's only brother, made a futile struggle for power, and freedom of choice in marriage, but was soon overcome. He was spared, as being the only heir to the kingdom, but the Duke of Montmorency, who had been led into his rebellion, was brought to the block, amid the pity and terror of all France. Whoever seemed dangerous to the State, or showed any spirit of independence, was marked by the cardinal, and suffered a hopeless imprisonment, if nothing worse; but at the same time his government was intelligent and able, and promoted prosperity, as far as was possible where there was such a crushing of individual spirit and enterprise. Richelieu's plan, in fact, was to found a despotism, though a wise and well-ordered despotism, at home, while he made France great by conquests abroad. And at this time the ambition of France found a favourable field in the state both of Germany and of Spain.

2. The War in Flanders and Italy. — The Thirty Years' War had been raging in Germany for many

years, and France had taken no part in it, beyond encouraging the Swedes and the Protestant Germans, as the enemies of the Emperor. But the policy of Richelieu required that the disunion between its Catholic and Protestant states should be maintained, and when things began to tend towards peace from mutual exhaustion, the cardinal interfered, and induced the Protestant party to continue the war by giving them money and reinforcements. A war had already begun in Italy on behalf of the Duke of Nevers, who had become heir to the duchy of Mantua, but whose family had lived in France so long that the Emperor and the King of Spain supported a more distant claim of the Duke of Savoy to part of the duchy, rather than admit a French prince into Italy. Richelieu was quick to seize this pretext for attacking Spain, for Spain was now dying into a weak power, and he saw in the war a means of acquiring the Netherlands, which belonged to the Spanish crown. At first nothing important was done, but the Spaniards and Germans were worn out, while two young and able captains were growing up among the French — the Viscount of Turenne, younger son to the Duke of Bouillon, and the Duke of Enghien, eldest son of the Prince of Condé — and Richelieu's policy soon secured a brilliant career of success. Elsass, Lorraine, Artois, Catalonia, and Savoy, all fell into the hands of the French, and from a chamber of sickness the cardinal directed the affairs of three armies, as well as made himself feared and respected by the whole kingdom. Cinq Mars, the last favourite he had given the king, plotted his overthrow, with the help of the Spaniards, but was detected and executed, when the great minister was already at death's door. Richelieu recommended an Italian priest, Julius Mazarin, whom he had trained to work under him, to carry on the government, and died in the December of 1642. The king only survived him five months, dying on the 14th of May, 1643. The war was continued on the lines Richelieu had laid down, and four days after the death of Louis XIII. the army in the Low Countries gained a splendid victory at Rocroy, under the Duke of Enghien, entirely destroying the old Spanish infantry. The battles of Freiburg, Nordlingen, and Lens raised the fame of the French generals to the highest pitch, and in 1649 reduced the Emperor to make peace in the treaty of Münster. France obtained as her spoil the three bishoprics, Metz, Toul, and Verdun, ten cities in Elsass, Brisach, and the Sundgau, with the Savoyard town of Pignerol; but the war with Spain continued till 1659, when Louis XIV. engaged to marry Maria Theresa, a daughter of the King of Spain.

3. The Fronde. — When an heir had long been despaired of, Anne of Austria, the wife of Louis XIII., had become the mother of two sons, the eldest of whom, *Louis XIV.*, was only five years old at the time of his father's death. The queen-mother became regent, and trusted entirely to Mazarin, who had become a cardinal, and pursued the policy of Richelieu. But what had been endured from a man by birth a French noble, was intolerable from a low-born Italian. "After the lion comes the fox," was the saying, and the Parliament of Paris made a last stand by refusing to register the royal edict for fresh taxes, being supported both by the burghers of Paris, and by a great number of the nobility, who were personally jealous of Mazarin. This party was called the Fronde, because in their discussions each man stood forth, launched his speech, and retreated, just as the boys did with slings (*fronde*) and stones in the streets. The struggle became serious, but only a few of the lawyers in the parliament had any real principle or public spirit; all

the other actors caballed out of jealousy and party spirit, making tools of "the men of the gown," whom they hated and despised, though mostly far their superiors in worth and intelligence. Anne of Austria held fast by Mazarin, and was supported by the Duke of Enghien, whom his father's death had made Prince of Condé. Condé's assistance enabled her to blockade Paris and bring the parliament to terms, which concluded the first act of the Fronde, with the banishment of Mazarin as a peace offering. Condé, however, became so arrogant and overbearing that the queen caused him to be imprisoned, whereupon his wife and his other friends began a fresh war for his liberation, and the queen was forced to yield; but he again showed himself so tyrannical that the queen and the parliament became reconciled and united to put him down, giving the command of the troops to Turenne. Again there was a battle at the gates of Paris, in which all Condé's friends were wounded, and he himself so entirely worsted that he had to go into exile, when he entered the Spanish service, while Mazarin returned to power at home.

4. The Court of Anne of Austria. — The court of France, though never pure, was much improved during the reign of Louis XIII. and the regency of Anne of Austria. There was a spirit of romance and grace about it, somewhat cumbrous and stately, but outwardly pure and refined, and quite a step out of the gross and open vice of the former reigns. The Duchess de Rambouillet, a lady of great grace and wit, made her house the centre of a brilliant society, which set itself to raise and refine the manners, literature, and language of the time. No word that was considered vulgar or coarse was allowed to pass muster; and though in process of time this censorship became pedantic and petty, there is no doubt that much was

done to purify both the language and the tone of thought. Poems, plays, epigrams, eulogiums, and even sermons were rehearsed before the committee of taste in the Hôtel de Rambouillet, and a wonderful new stimulus was there given, not only to ornamental but to solid literature. Many of the great men who made France illustrious were either ending or beginning their careers at this time. Memoir writing specially flourished, and the characters of the men and women of the court are known to us on all sides. Cardinal de Retz and the Duke of Rochefoucauld, both deeply engaged in the Fronde, have left, the one memoirs, the other maxims of great power of irony. Mme. de Motteville, one of the queen's ladies, wrote a full history of the court. Blaise Pascal, one of the greatest geniuses of all times, was attaching himself to the Jansenists. This religious party, so called from Jansen, a Dutch priest, whose opinions were imputed to them, had sprung up around the reformed convent of Port Royal, and numbered among them some of the ablest and best men of the time; but the Jesuits considered them to hold false doctrine, and there was a continual debate, ending at length in the persecution of the Jansenists. Pascal's "Provincial Letters," exposing the Jesuit system, were among the ablest writings of the age. Philosophy, poetry, science, history, art, were all making great progress, though there was a stateliness and formality in all that was said and done, redolent of the Spanish queen's etiquette and the fastidious refinement of the Hôtel Rambouillet.

5. Court of Louis XIV. — The attempt from the earliest times of the French monarchy had been to draw all government into the hands of the sovereign, and the suppression of the Fronde completed the work. Louis XIV., though ill educated, was a man of considerable ability, much industry, and great force of

character, arising from a profound belief that France was the first country in the world, and himself the first of Frenchmen; and he had a magnificent courtesy of demeanour, which so impressed all who came near him as to make them his willing slaves. "There is enough in him to make four kings and one respectable man besides" was what Mazarin said of him; and when in 1661 the cardinal died, the king showed himself fully equal to becoming his own prime minister. "The State is myself," he said, and all centred upon him so that no room was left for statesmen. The court was, however, in a most brilliant state. There had been an unusual outburst of talent of every kind in the lull after the Wars of Religion, and in generals, thinkers, artists, and men of literature, France was unusually rich. The king had a wonderful power of self-assertion, which attached them all to him almost as if he were a sort of divinity. The stately, elaborate Spanish etiquette brought in by his mother, Anne of Austria, became absolutely an engine of government. Henry IV. had begun the evil custom of keeping the nobles quiet by giving them situations at court, with pensions attached, and these offices were multiplied to the most enormous and absurd degree, so that every royal personage had some hundreds of personal attendants. Princes of the blood and nobles of every degree were contented to hang about the court, crowding into the most narrow lodgings at Versailles, and thronging its anterooms; and to be ordered to remain in the country was a most severe punishment.

6. France under Louis XIV. — There was, in fact, nothing but the chase to occupy a gentleman on his own estate, for he was allowed no duties or responsibilities. Each province had a governor or *intendant*, a sort of viceroy, and the administration of the cities was managed chiefly on the part of the king, even the

mayors obtaining their posts by purchase. The unhappy peasants had to pay in the first place the taxes to Government, out of which were defrayed an intolerable number of pensions, many for useless offices; next, the rents and dues which supported their lord's expenditure at court; and, thirdly, the tithes and fees of the clergy. Besides which, they were called off from the cultivation of their own fields for a certain number of days to work at the roads; their horses might be used by royal messengers; their lord's crops had to be got in by their labour gratis, while their own were spoiling; and, in short, the only wonder is how they existed at all. Their hovels and their food were wretched, and any attempt to amend their condition on the part of their lord would have been looked on as betokening dangerous designs, and probably have landed him in the Bastille. The peasants of Brittany — where the old constitution had been less entirely ruined — and those of Anjou were in a less oppressed condition, and in the cities trade flourished. Colbert, the comptroller-general of the finances, was so excellent a manager that the pressure of taxation was endurable in his time, and he promoted new manufactures, such as glass at Cherbourg, cloth at Abbeville, silk at Lyons; he also tried to promote commerce and colonization, and to create a navy. There was a great appearance of prosperity, and in every department there was wonderful ability. The Reformation had led to a considerable revival among the Roman Catholics themselves. The theological colleges established in the last reign had much improved the tone of the clergy. Bossuet, Bishop of Meaux, was one of the most noted preachers who ever existed, and Fénélon, Archbishop of Cambrai, one of the best of men. A reform of discipline, begun in the convent of Port Royal, ended by attracting and gathering together some of the most excellent and able persons in France — among them Blaise Pascal, a man of marvellous genius and depth of thought, and Racine, the chief French dramatic poet. Their chief director, the Abbot of St. Cyran, was however, a pupil of Jansen, a Dutch ecclesiastic, whose views on abstruse questions of grace were condemned by the Jesuits; and as the Port-Royalists would not disown the doctrines attributed to him, they were discouraged and persecuted throughout Louis's reign, more because he was jealous of what would not bend to his will than for any real want of conformity. Pascal's famous "Provincial Letters" were put forth during this controversy; and in fact, the literature of France reached its Augustan age during this reign, and the language acquired its standard perfection.

7. War in the Low Countries. — Maria Theresa, the queen of Louis XIV., was the child of the first marriage of Philip IV. of Spain; and on her father's death in 1661, Louis, on pretext of an old law in Brabant, which gave the daughters of a first marriage the preference over the sons of a second, claimed the Low Countries from the young Charles II. of Spain. He thus began a war which was really a continuance of the old struggle between France and Burgundy, and of the endeavour of France to stretch her frontier to the Rhine. At first England, Holland, and Sweden united against him, and obliged him to make the peace of Aix-la-Chapelle in 1668; but he then succeeded in bribing Charles II. of England to forsake the cause of the Dutch, and the war was renewed in 1672. William, Prince of Orange, Louis's most determined enemy through life, kept up the spirits of the Dutch, and they obtained aid from Germany and Spain, through a six years' terrible war, in which the great Turenne was killed at Saltzbach, in Germany. At last,

from exhaustion, all parties were compelled to conclude the peace of Nimeguen in 1678. Taking advantage of undefined terms in this treaty, Louis seized various cities belonging to German princes, and likewise the free imperial city of Strassburg, when all Germany was too much worn out by the long war to offer resistance. France was full of self-glorification, the king was viewed almost as a demi-god, and the splendour of his court and of his buildings, especially the palace at Versailles, with its gardens and fountains, kept up the delusion of his greatness.

8. Revocation of the Edict of Nantes. — In 1685 Louis supposed that the Huguenots had been so reduced in numbers that the Edict of Nantes could be repealed. All freedom of worship was denied them; their ministers were banished, but their flocks were not allowed to follow them. If taken while trying to escape, men were sent to the galleys, women to captivity, and children to convents for education. Dragoons were quartered on families to torment them into going to mass. A few made head in the wild moors of the Cevennes under a brave youth named Cavalier, and others endured severe persecution in the south of France. Dragoons were quartered on them, who made it their business to torment and insult them; their marriages were declared invalid, their children taken from them to be educated in the Roman Catholic faith. A great number, amounting to at least 100,000, succeeded in escaping, chiefly to Prussia, Holland, and England, whither they carried many of the manufactures that Colbert had taken so much pains to establish. Many of those who settled in England were silk weavers, and a large colony was thus established at Spitalfields, which long kept up its French character.

9. The War of the Palatinate. — This brutal act of tyranny was followed by a fresh attack on Germany. On the plea of a supposed inheritance of his sister-in-law, the Duchess of Orleans, Louis invaded the Palatinate on the Rhine, and carried on one of the most ferocious wars in history, while he was at the same time supporting the cause of his cousin, James II. of England, after he had fled and abdicated on the arrival of William of Orange. During this war, however, that generation of able men who had grown up with Louis began to pass away, and his success was not so uniform; while, Colbert being dead, taxation began to be more felt by the exhausted people, and peace was made at Ryswick in 1697.

10. The War of the Succession in Spain. — The last of the four great wars of Louis's reign was far more unfortunate. Charles II. of Spain died childless, naming as his successor a French prince, Philip, Duke of Anjou, the second son of the only son of Charles's eldest sister, the queen of Louis XIV. But the Powers of Europe, at the Peace of Ryswick, had agreed that the crown of Spain should go to Charles of Austria, second son of the Emperor Leopold, who was the descendant of younger sisters of the royal Spanish line, but did not excite the fear and jealousy of Europe, as did a scion of the already overweening house of Bourbon. This led to the War of the Spanish Succession, England and Holland supporting Charles, and fighting with Louis in Spain, Savoy, and the Low Countries. In Spain Louis was ultimately successful, and his grandson Philip V. retained the throne; but the troops which his ally, the Elector of Bavaria, introduced into Germany were totally overthrown at Blenheim by the English army under the Duke of Marlborough, and the Austrian under Prince Eugene, a son of a younger branch of the house of Savoy.

Eugene had been bred up in France, but, having bitterly offended Louis by calling him a stage king for show and a chess king for use, had entered the Emperor's service, and was one of his chief enemies. He aided his cousin, Duke Victor Amadeus of Savoy, in repulsing the French attacks in that quarter, gained a great victory at Turin, and advanced into Provence. Marlborough was likewise in full career of victory in the Low Countries, and gained there the battle of Ramillies.

11. Peace of Utrecht. — Louis had outlived his good fortune. His great generals and statesmen had passed away. The country was exhausted, famine was preying on the wretched peasantry, supplies could not be found, and one city after another, of those Louis had seized, was retaken. New victories at Oudenarde and Malplaquet were gained over the French armies; and, though Louis was as resolute and undaunted as ever, his affairs were in a desperate state, when he was saved by a sudden change of policy on the part of Queen Anne of England, who recalled her army and left her allies to continue the contest alone. Eugene was not a match for France without Marlborough, and the Archduke Charles, having succeeded his brother the Emperor, gave up his pretensions to the crown of Spain, so that it became possible to conclude a general peace at Utrecht in 1713. By this time Louis was seventy-five years of age, and had suffered grievous family losses — first by the death of his only son, and then of his eldest grandson, a young man of much promise of excellence, who, with his wife died of malignant measles, probably from ignorant medical treatment, since their infant, whose illness was concealed by his nurses, was the only one of the family who survived. The old king, in spite of sorrow and reverse, toiled with indomitable energy to

the end of his reign, the longest on record, having lasted seventy-two years, when he died in 1715. He had raised the French crown to its greatest splendour, but had sacrificed the country to himself and his false notions of greatness.

12. The Regency. — The crown now descended to *Louis XV.*, a weakly child of four years old. His great-grandfather had tried to provide for his good by leaving the chief seat in the council of regency to his own illegitimate son, the Duke of Maine, the most honest and conscientious man then in the family, but, though clever, unwise and very unpopular. His birth caused the appointment to be viewed as an outrage by the nobility, and the king's will was set aside. The first prince of the blood royal, Philip, Duke of Orleans, the late king's nephew, became sole regent — a man of good ability, but of easy, indolent nature; and who, in the enforced idleness of his life, had become dissipated and vicious beyond all imagination or description. He was kindly and gracious, and his mother said of him that he was like the prince in a fable whom all the fairies had endowed with gifts, except one malignant sprite who had prevented any favour being of use to him. In the general exhaustion produced by the wars of Louis XIV., a Scotchman named James Law began the great system of hollow speculation which has continued ever since to tempt people to their ruin. He tried raising sums of money on national credit, and also devised a company who were to lend money to found a great settlement on the Mississippi, the returns from which were to be enormous. Every one speculated in shares, and the wildest excitement prevailed. Law's house was mobbed by people seeking interviews with him, and nobles disguised themselves in liveries to get access to him. Fortunes were made one week and lost the next, and finally the whole plan

proved to have been a mere baseless scheme; ruin followed, and the misery of the country increased. The Duke of Orleans died suddenly in 1723. The king was now legally of age; but he was dull and backward, and little fitted for government, and the country was really ruled by the Duke of Bourbon, and after him by Cardinal Fleury, an aged statesman, but filled with the same schemes of ambition as Richelieu or Mazarin.

13. War of the Austrian Succession. — Thus France plunged into new wars. Louis XV. married the daughter of Stanislas Lecksinsky, a Polish noble, who, after being raised to the throne, was expelled by Austrian intrigues and violence. Louis was obliged to take up arms on behalf of his father-in-law, but was bought off by a gift from the Emperor Charles VI. of the duchy of Lorraine to Stanislas, to revert to his daughter after his death and thus become united to France. Lorraine belonged to Duke Francis, the husband of Maria Theresa, eldest daughter to the Emperor, and Francis received instead the duchy of Tuscany; while all the chief Powers in Europe agreed to the so-called Pragmatic Sanction, by which Charles decreed that Maria Theresa should inherit Austria and Hungary and the other hereditary states on her father's death, to the exclusion of the daughters of his elder brother, Joseph. When Charles VI. died, however, in 1740, a great European war began on this matter. Frederick II. of Prussia would neither allow Maria Theresa's claim to the hereditary states, nor join in electing her husband to the Empire; and France took part against her, sending Marshal Belleisle to support the Elector of Bavaria, who had been chosen Emperor. George II. of England held with Maria Theresa, and gained a victory over the French at Dettingen, in 1744. Louis XV. then joined his army, and the

battle of Fontenoy, in 1745, was one of the rare victories of France over England. Another victory followed at Laufeldt, but elsewhere France had had heavy losses, and in 1748, after the death of Charles VII., peace was made at Aix-la-Chapelle.

14. The Seven Years' War. — Louis, dull and selfish by nature, had been absolutely led into vice by his courtiers, especially the Duke of Bourbon, who feared his becoming active in public affairs. He had no sense of duty to his people; and whereas his great-grandfather had sought display and so-called glory, he cared solely for pleasure, and that of the grossest and most sensual order, so that his court was a hotbed of shameless vice. All that could be wrung from the impoverished country was lavished on the overgrown establishments of every member of the royal family, in pensions to nobles, and in shameful amusements of the king. In 1756 another war broke out, in consequence of the hatreds left between Prussia and Austria by the former struggle. Maria Theresa had, by flatteries she ought to have disdained, gained over France to take part with her, and England was allied with Frederick II. In this war France and England chiefly fought in their distant possessions, where the English were uniformly successful; and after seven years another peace followed, leaving the boundaries of the German states just where they were before, after a frightful amount of bloodshed. But France had had terrible losses. She was driven from India, and lost all her settlements in America and Canada.

15. France under Louis XV. — Meantime the gross vice and licentiousness of the king was beyond description, and the nobility retained about the court by the system established by Louis XIV. were, if not his equals in crime, equally callous to the suffering

caused by the reckless expensiveness of the court, the whole cost of which was defrayed by the burghers and peasants. No taxes were asked from clergy or nobles, and this latter term included all sprung of a noble line to the utmost generation. The owner of an estate had no means of benefiting his tenants, even if he wished it; for all matters, even of local government, depended on the crown. All he could do was to draw his income from them, and he was often forced, either by poverty or by his expensive life, to strain to the utmost the old feudal system. If he lived at court, his expenses were heavy, and only partly met by his pension, likewise raised from the taxes paid by the poor farmer; if he lived in the country, he was a still greater tyrant, and was called by the people a *hobereau*, or kite. No career was open to his younger sons, except in the court, the Church, or the army, and here they monopolized the prizes, obtaining all the richer dioceses and abbeys, and all the promotion in the army. The magistracies were almost all hereditary among lawyers, who had bought them for their families from the crown, and paid for the appointment of each son. The officials attached to each member of the royal family were almost incredible in number, and all paid by the taxes. The old *gabelle*, or salt-tax, had gone on ever since the English wars, and every member of a family had to pay it, not according to what they used, but what they were supposed to need. Every pig was rated at what he ought to require for salting. Every cow, sheep, or hen had a toll to pay to king, lord, bishop — sometimes also to priest and abbey. The peasant was called off from his own work to give the dues of labour to the roads or to his lord. He might not spread manure that could interfere with the game, nor drive away the partridges that ate his corn. So scanty were his crops that famines slaying thousands passed unnoticed, and even if, by any wonder, prosperity smiled on the peasant, he durst not live in any kind of comfort, lest the stewards of his lord or of Government should pounce on his wealth.

16. Reaction. — Meantime there was a strong feeling that change must come. Classical literature was studied, and Greek and Roman manners and institutions were thought ideal perfection. There was great disgust at the fetters of a highly artificial life in which every one was bound, and at the institutions which had been so misused. Writers arose, among whom Voltaire and Rousseau were the most eminent, who aimed at the overthrow of all the ideas which had come to be thus abused. The one by his caustic wit, the other by his enthusiastic simplicity, gained willing ears, and, the writers in a great Encyclopædia then in course of publication, contrived to attack most of the notions which had been hitherto taken for granted, and were closely connected with faith and with government. The king himself was dully aware that he was living on the crust of a volcano, but he said it would last his time; and so it did. Louis XV. died of smallpox in 1774, leaving his grandsons to reap the harvest that generations had been sowing.

CHAPTER VII.

THE REVOLUTION.

1. Attempts at Reform. — It was evident that a change must be made. *Louis XVI.* himself knew it, and slurred over the words in his coronation oath that bound him to extirpate heresy; but he was a slow, dull man, and affairs had come to such a pass that a far abler man than he could hardly have dealt with the dead-lock above, without causing a frightful outbreak of the pent-up masses below. His queen, Marie Antoinette, was hated for being of Austrian birth, and, though a spotless and noble woman, her most trivial actions gave occasion to calumnies founded on the crimes of the last generation. Unfortunately, the king, though an honest and well-intentioned man, was totally unfit to guide a country through a dangerous crisis. His courage was passive, his manners were heavy, dull, and shy, and, though steadily industrious, he was slow of comprehension and unready in action; and reformation was the more difficult because to abolish the useless court offices would have been utter starvation to many of their holders, who had nothing but their pensions to live upon. Yet there was a general passion for reform; all ranks alike looked to some change to free them from the deadlock which made improvement impossible. The Government was bankrupt, while the taxes were intolerable, and the first years of the reign were spent in experiments. Necker, a Swiss banker, was invited to take the charge of the finances, and large loans were made to Government, for which he contrived to pay interest regularly; some reduction was made in the expenditure; but the king's old minister, Maurepas, grew jealous of his popularity, and obtained his dis-

missal. The French took the part of the American colonies in their revolt from England, and the war thus occasioned brought on an increase of the load of debt, the general distress increased, and it became necessary to devise some mode of taxing which might divide the burthens between the whole nation, instead of making the peasants pay all and the nobles and clergy nothing. Louis decided on calling together the Notables, or higher nobility; but they were by no means disposed to tax themselves, and only abused his ministers. He then resolved on convoking the whole States-General of the kingdom, which had never met since the reign of Louis XIII.

2. The States-General. — No one exactly knew the limits of the powers of the States-General when it met in 1789. Nobles, clergy, and the deputies who represented the commonalty, all formed the assembly at Versailles; and though the king would have kept apart these last, who were called the *Tiers Etât*, or third estate, they refused to withdraw from the great hall of Versailles. The Count of Mirabeau, the younger son of a noble family, who sat as a deputy, declared that nothing short of bayonets should drive out those who sat by the will of the people, and Louis yielded. Thenceforth the votes of a noble, a bishop, or a deputy all counted alike. The party names of democrat for those who wanted to exalt the power of the people, and of aristocrat for those who maintained the privileges of the nobles, came into use, and the most extreme democrats were called Jacobins, from an old convent of Jacobin friars, where they used to meet. The mob of Paris, always eager, fickle, and often blood-thirsty, were excited to the last degree by the debates; and, full of the remembrance of the insolence and cruelty of the nobles, sometimes rose and hunted down persons whom they deemed aristocrats, hang-

ing them to the iron rods by which lamps were suspended over the streets. The king in alarm drew the army nearer, and it was supposed that he was going to prevent all change by force of arms. Thereupon the citizens enrolled themselves as a National Guard, wearing cockades of red, blue, and white, and commanded by La Fayette, a noble of democratic opinions, who had run away at seventeen to serve in the American War. On a report that the cannon of the Bastille had been pointed upon Paris, the mob rose in a frenzy, rushed upon it, hanged the guard, and absolutely tore down the old castle to its foundations, though they did not find a single prisoner in it. "This is a revolt," said Louis, when he heard of it. "Sire, it is a revolution," was the answer.

3. The New Constitution. — The mob had found out its power. The fishwomen of the markets, always a peculiar and privileged class, were frantically excited, and were sure to be foremost in all the demonstrations stirred up by Jacobins. There was a great scarcity of provisions in Paris, and this, together with the continual dread that reforms would be checked by violence, maddened the people. On a report that the Guards had shown enthusiasm for the king, the whole populace came pouring out of Paris to Versailles, and, after threatening the life of the queen, brought the family back with them to Paris, and kept them almost as prisoners while the Assembly, which followed them to Paris, debated on the new constitution. The nobles were viewed as the worst enemies of the nation, and all over the country there were risings of the peasants, headed by democrats from the towns, who sacked their castles, and often seized their persons. Many fled to England and Germany, and the dread that these would unite and return to bring back the old system continually increased the fury of the peo-

ple. The Assembly, now known as the Constituent Assembly, swept away all titles and privileges, and no one was henceforth to bear any prefix to his name but citizen; while at the same time the clergy were to renounce all the property of the Church, and to swear that their office and commission was derived from the will of the people alone, and that they owed no obedience save to the State. The estates thus yielded up were supposed to be enough to supply all State expenses without taxes; but as they could not at once be turned into money, promissory notes, or assignats, were issued. But, as coin was scarce, these were not worth nearly their professed value, and the general distress was thus much increased. The other oath the great body of the clergy utterly refused, and they were therefore driven out of their benefices, and became objects of great suspicion to the democrats. All the old boundaries and other distinctions between the provinces were destroyed, and France was divided into departments, each of which was to elect deputies, in whose assembly all power was to be vested, except that the king retained a right of veto, *i.e.*, of refusing his sanction to any measure. He swore on the 13th of August, 1791, to observe this new constitution.

4. The Republic. — The Constituent Assembly now dissolved itself, and a fresh Assembly, called the Legislative, took its place. For a time things went on more peacefully. Distrust was, however, deeply sown. The king was closely watched as an enemy; and those of the nobles who had emigrated began to form armies, aided by the Germans, on the frontier for his rescue. This enraged the people, who expected that their newly won liberties would be overthrown. The first time the king exercised his right of *veto* the mob rose in fury; and though they then did no more than threaten, on the advance of the emigrant army on the

10th of August, 1792, a more terrible rising took place. The Tuilleries was sacked, the guards slaughtered, the unresisting king and his family deposed and imprisoned in the tower of the Temple. In terror lest the nobles in the prisons should unite with the emigrants, they were massacred by wholesale; while, with a vigour born of the excitement, the emigrant armies were repulsed and beaten. The monarchy came to an end; and France became a Republic, in which the National Convention, which followed the Legislative Assembly, was supreme. The more moderate members of this were called Girondins from the Gironde, the estuary of the Garonne, from the neighbourhood of which many of them came. They were able men, scholars and philosophers, full of schemes for reviving classical times, but wishing to stop short of the plans of the Jacobins, of whom the chief was Robespierre, a lawyer from Artois, filled with fanatical notions of the rights of man. He, with a party of other violent republicans, called the Mountain, of whom Danton and Marat were most noted, set to work to destroy all that interfered with their plans of general equality. The guillotine, a recently invented machine for beheading, was set in all the chief market-places, and hundreds were put to death on the charge of "conspiring against the nation." Louis XVI. was executed early in 1793; and it was enough to have any sort of birthright to be thought dangerous and put to death.

5. The Reign of Terror. — Horror at the bloodshed perpetrated by the Mountain led a young girl, named Charlotte Corday, to assassinate Marat, whom she supposed to be the chief cause of the cruelties that were taking place; but his death only added to the dread of reaction. A Committee of Public Safety was appointed by the Convention, and endeavoured to sweep away every being who either seemed adverse

to equality, or who might inherit any claim to rank. The queen was put to death nine months after her husband; and the Girondins, who had begun to try to stem the tide of slaughter, soon fell under the denunciation of the more violent. To be accused of "conspiring against the State" was instantly fatal, and no one's life was safe. Danton was denounced by Robespierre, and perished; and for three whole years the Reign of Terror lasted. The emigrants, by forming an army and advancing on France, assisted by the forces of Germany, only made matters worse. There was such a dread of the old oppressions coming back, that the peasants were ready to fight to the death against the return of the nobles. The army, where promotion used to go by rank instead of merit, were so glad of the change, that they were full of fresh spirit, and repulsed the army of Germans and emigrants all along the frontier. The city of Lyons, which had tried to resist the changes, was taken, and frightfully used by Collot d'Herbois, a member of the Committee of Public Safety. The guillotine was too slow for him, and he had the people mown down with grape-shot, declaring that of this great city nothing should be left but a monument inscribed, "Lyons resisted liberty — Lyons is no more!" In La Vendée — a district of Anjou, where the peasants were much attached to their clergy and nobles — they rose and gained such successes, that they dreamt for a little while of rescuing and restoring the little captive son of Louis XVI.; but they were defeated and put down by fire and sword, and at Nantes an immense number of executions took place, chiefly by drowning. It was reckoned that no less than 18,600 persons were guillotined in the three years between 1790 and 1794, besides those who died by other means. Everything was changed. Religion was to be done away with; the churches were closed;

the tenth instead of the seventh day appointed for rest. "Death is an eternal sleep" was inscribed on the schools; and Reason, represented by a classically dressed woman, was enthroned in the cathedral of Notre Dâme. At the same time a new era was invented, the 22nd of September, 1792; the months had new names, and the decimal measures of length, weight, and capacity, which are based on the proportions of the earth, were planned. All this time Robespierre really seems to have thought himself the benefactor of the human race; but at last the other members of the Convention took courage to denounce him, and he, with five more, was arrested and sent to the guillotine. The bloodthirsty fever was over, the Committee of Public Safety was overthrown, and people breathed again.

6. The Directory. — The chief executive power was placed in the hands of a Directory, consisting of more moderate men, and a time of much prosperity set in. Already in the new vigour born of the strong emotions of the country the armies won great victories, not only repelling the Germans and the emigrants, but uniting Holland to France. Napoleon Buonaparte, a Corsican officer, who was called on to protect the Directory from being again overawed by the mob, became the leading spirit in France, through his Italian victories. He conquered Lombardy and Tuscany, and forced the Emperor to let them become republics under French protection, also to resign Flanders to France by the Treaty of Campo Formio. Buonaparte then made a descent on Egypt, hoping to attack India from that side, but he was foiled by Nelson, who destroyed his fleet in the battle of the Nile, and Sir Sydney Smith, who held out Acre against him. He hurried home to France on finding that the Directory had begun a fresh European war, seizing Swit-

zerland, and forcing it to give up its treasures and become a republic on their model, and carrying the Pope off into captivity. All the European Powers had united against them, and Lombardy had been recovered chiefly by Russian aid; so that Buonaparte, on the ground that a nation at war needed a less cumbrous government than a Directory, contrived to get himself chosen First Consul, with two inferiors, in 1799.

7. The Consulate. — A great course of victories followed in Italy, where Buonaparte commanded in person, and in Germany under Moreau. Austria and Russia were forced to make peace, and England was the only country that still resisted him, till a general peace was made at Amiens in 1803; but it only lasted for a year, for the French failed to perform the conditions, and began the war afresh. In the mean time Buonaparte had restored religion and order, and so entirely mastered France that, in 1804, he was able to form the republic into an empire, and affecting to be another Charles the Great, he caused the Pope to say mass at his coronation, though he put the crown on his own head. A concordat with the Pope reinstated the clergy, but altered the division of the dioceses, and put the bishops and priests in the pay of the State.

8. The Empire. — The union of Italy to this new French Empire caused a fresh war with all Europe. The Austrian army, however, was defeated at Ulm and Austerlitz, the Prussians were entirely crushed at Jena, and the Russians fought two terrible but almost drawn battles at Eylau and Friedland. Peace was then made with all three at Tilsit, in 1807, the terms pressing exceedingly hard upon Prussia. Schemes of invading England were entertained by the Emperor, but were disconcerted by the destruction of the French and Spanish fleets by Nelson at Trafalgar. Spain was

then in alliance with France; but Napoleon, treacherously getting the royal family into his hands, seized their kingdom, making his brother Joseph its king. But the Spaniards would not submit, and called in the English to their aid. The Peninsular War resulted in a series of victories on the part of the English under Wellington, while Austria, beginning another war, was again so crushed that the Emperor durst not refuse to give his daughter in marriage to Napoleon. However, in 1812, the conquest of Russia proved an exploit beyond Napoleon's powers. He reached Moscow with his Grand Army, but the city was burnt down immediately after his arrival, and he had no shelter or means of support. He was forced to retreat, through a fearful winter, without provisions and harassed by the Cossacks, who hung on the rear and cut off the stragglers, so that his whole splendid army had become a mere miserable, broken, straggling remnant by the time the survivors reached the Prussian frontier. He himself had hurried back to Paris as soon as he found their case hopeless, to arrange his resistance to all Europe — for every country rose against him on his first disaster — and the next year was spent in a series of desperate battles in Germany between him and the Allied Powers. Lützen and Bautzen were doubtful, but the two days' battle of Leipzic was a terrible defeat. In the year 1814, four armies — those of Austria, Russia, England, and Prussia — entered France at once; and though Napoleon resisted, stood bravely and skilfully, and gained single battles against Austria and Prussia, he could not stand against all Europe. In April the Allies entered Paris, and he was forced to abdicate, being sent under a strong guard to the little Mediterranean isle of Elba. He had drained France of men by his constant call for soldiers, who were drawn by conscription from the whole country, till there were not enough to do the work in the fields, and foreign prisoners had to be employed; but he had conferred on her one great benefit in the great code of laws called the "*Code Napoléon*," which has ever since continued in force.

9. France under Napoleon. — The old laws and customs, varying in different provinces, had been swept away, so that the field was clear; and the system of government which Napoleon devised has remained practically unchanged from that time to this. Everything was made to depend upon the central government. The Ministers of Religion, of Justice, of Police, of Education, etc., have the regulation of all interior affairs, and appoint all who work under them, so that nobody learns how to act alone; and as the Government has been in fact ever since dependent on the will of the people of Paris, the whole country is helplessly in their hands. The army, as in almost all foreign nations, is raised by conscription — that is, by drawing lots among the young men liable to serve, and who can only escape by paying a substitute to serve in their stead; and this is generally the first object of the savings of a family. All feudal claims had been done away with, and with them the right of primogeniture; and, indeed, it is not possible for a testator to avoid leaving his property to be shared among his family, though he can make some small differences in the amount each receives, and thus estates are continually freshly divided, and some portions become very small indeed. French peasants are, however, most eager to own land, and are usually very frugal, sober, and saving; and the country has gone on increasing in prosperity and comfort. It is true that, probably from the long habit of concealing any wealth they might possess, the French farmers and peasantry care little for display, or what we should call comfort,

and live rough hard-working lives even while well off and with large hoards of wealth; but their condition has been wonderfully changed for the better ever since the Revolution. All this has continued under the numerous changes that have taken place in the forms of government.

CHAPTER VIII.

FRANCE SINCE THE REVOLUTION.

1. The Restoration. — The Allies left the people of France free to choose their Government, and they accepted the old royal family, who were on their borders awaiting a recall. The son of Louis XVI. had perished in the hands of his jailers, and thus the king's next brother, *Louis XVIII.*, succeeded to the throne, bringing back a large emigrant following. Things were not settled down, when Napoleon, in the spring of 1815, escaped from Elba. The army welcomed him with delight, and Louis was forced to flee to Ghent. However, the Allies immediately rose in arms, and the troops of England and Prussia crushed Napoleon entirely at Waterloo, on the 18th of June, 1815. He was sent to the lonely rock of St. Helena, in the Atlantic, whence he could not again return to trouble the peace of Europe. There he died in 1821. Louis XVIII. was restored, and a charter was devised by which a limited monarchy was established, a king at the head, and two chambers — one of peers, the other of deputies, but with a very narrow franchise. It did not, however, work amiss; till, after Louis's death in 1824, his brother, *Charles X.*, tried to fall back on the old system. He checked the freedom of the press, and interfered with the freedom of elections. The consequence was a fresh revolution in July, 1830, happily with little bloodshed, but which forced Charles X. to go into exile with his grandchild Henry, whose father, the Duke of Berry, had been assassinated in 1820.

2. Reign of Louis Philippe. — The chambers of deputies offered the crown to *Louis Philippe*, Duke of Orleans. He was descended from the regent; his father had been one of the democratic party in the Revolu-

tion, and, when titles were abolished, had called himself Philip *Egalité* (Equality). This had not saved his head under the Reign of Terror, and his son had been obliged to flee and lead a wandering life, at one time gaining his livelihood by teaching mathematics at a school in Switzerland. He had recovered his family estates at the Restoration, and, as the head of the Liberal party, was very popular. He was elected King of the French, not of France, with a chamber of peers nominated for life only, and another of deputies elected by voters, whose qualification was two hundred francs, or eight pounds a year. He did his utmost to gain the good will of the people, living a simple, friendly family life, and trying to merit the term of the "citizen king," and in the earlier years of his reign he was successful. The country was prosperous, and a great colony was settled in Algiers, and endured a long and desperate war with the wild Arab tribes. A colony was also established in New Caledonia, in the Pacific, and attempts were carried out to compensate thus for the losses of colonial possessions which France had sustained in wars with England. Discontents, however, began to arise, on the one hand from those who remembered only the successes of Buonaparte, and not the miseries they had caused, and on the other from the working-classes, who declared that the *bourgeois*, or tradespeople, had gained everything by the revolution of July, but they themselves nothing. Louis Philippe did his best to gratify and amuse the people by sending for the remains of Napoleon, and giving him a magnificent funeral and splendid monument among his old soldiers — the Invalides; but his popularity was waning. In 1842 his eldest son, the Duke of Orleans, a favourite with the people, was killed by a fall from his carriage, and this was another shock to his throne. Two young grandsons were left;

and the king had also several sons, one of whom, the Duke of Montpensier, he gave in marriage to Louise, the sister and heiress presumptive to the Queen of Spain; though, by treaty with the other European Powers, it had been agreed that she should not marry a French prince unless the queen had children of her own. Ambition for his family was a great offence to his subjects, and at the same time a nobleman, the Duke de Praslin, who had murdered his wife, committed suicide in prison to avoid public execution; and the republicans declared, whether justly or unjustly, that this had been allowed rather than let a noble die a felon's death.

3. The Revolution of 1848. — In spite of the increased prosperity of the country, there was general disaffection. There were four parties — the Orleanists, who held by Louis Philippe and his minister Guizot, and whose badge was the tricolour; the Legitimists, who retained their loyalty to the exiled Henry, and whose symbol was the white Bourbon flag; the Buonapartists; and the Republicans, whose badge was the red cap and flag. A demand for a franchise that should include the mass of the people was rejected, and the general displeasure poured itself out in speeches at political banquets. An attempt to stop one of these led to an uproar. The National Guard refused to fire on the people, and their fury rose unchecked; so that the king, thinking resistance vain, signed an abdication, and fled to England in February, 1848. A provisional Government was formed, and a new constitution was to be arranged; but the Paris mob, who found their condition unchanged, and really wanted equality of wealth, not of rights, made disturbances again and again, and barricaded the streets, till they were finally put down by General Cavaignac, while the rest of France was entirely dependent on the will

of the capital. After some months, a republic was determined on, which was to have a president at its head, chosen every five years by universal suffrage. Louis Napoleon Buonaparte, nephew to the great Napoleon, was the first president thus chosen; and, after some struggles, he not only mastered Paris, but, by the help of the army, which was mostly Buonapartist, he dismissed the chamber of deputies, and imprisoned or exiled all the opponents whom the troops had not put to death, on the plea of an expected rising of the mob. This was called a *coup d'état*, and Louis Napoleon was then declared president for ten years.

4. The Second Empire. — In December, 1852, the president took the title of Emperor, calling himself Napoleon III., as successor to the young son of the great Napoleon. He kept up a splendid and expensive court, made Paris more than ever the toy-shop of the world, and did much to improve it by the widening of streets and removal of old buildings. Treaties were made which much improved trade, and the country advanced in prosperity. The reins of government were, however, tightly held, and nothing was so much avoided as the letting men think or act for themselves, while their eyes were to be dazzled with splendour and victory. In 1853, when Russia was attacking Turkey, the Emperor united with England in opposition, and the two armies together besieged Sebastopol, and fought the battles of Alma and Inkermann, taking the city after nearly a year's siege; and then making what is known as the Treaty of Paris, which guaranteed the safety of Turkey so long as the subject Christian nations were not misused. In 1859 Napoleon III. joined in an attack on the Austrian power in Italy, and together with Victor Emanuel, King of Sardinia, and the Italians, gained two great victories at Magenta and Solferino; but made peace as

soon as it was convenient to him, without regard to his promises to the King of Sardinia, who was obliged to purchase his consent to becoming King of United Italy by yielding up to France his old inheritance of Savoy and Nice. Meantime discontent began to spring up at home, and the Red Republican spirit was working on. The huge fortunes made by the successful only added to the sense of contrast; secret societies were at work, and the Emperor, after twenty years of success, felt his popularity waning.

5. The Franco-German War. — In 1870 the Spaniards, who had deposed their queen, Isabel II., made choice of a relation of the King of Prussia as their king. There had long been bitter jealousy between France and Prussia, and, though the prince refused the offer of Spain, the French showed such an overbearing spirit that a war broke out. The real desire of France was to obtain the much-coveted frontier of the Rhine, and the Emperor heated their armies with boastful proclamations which were but the prelude to direful defeats, at Weissenburg, Wörth, and Forbach. At Sedan, the Emperor was forced to surrender himself as a prisoner, and the tidings no sooner arrived at Paris than the whole of the people turned their wrath on him and his family. His wife, the Empress Eugènie, had to flee, a republic was declared, and the city prepared to stand a siege. The Germans advanced, and put down all resistance in other parts of France. Great part of the army had been made prisoners, and, though there was much bravado, there was little steadiness or courage left among those who now took up arms. Paris, which was blockaded, after suffering much from famine, surrendered in February, 1871; and peace was purchased in a treaty by which great part of Elsass and Lorraine, and the city of Metz, were given back to Germany.

www.ingramcontent.com/pod-product-compliance
Lightning Source LLC
Chambersburg PA
CBHW020130010526
44115CB00008B/1054